The Unsearchable Riches of Christ

30 Days of Devotionals
Discovering God's Spiritual Treasures

by

Wayne Taylor

The Unsearchable Riches of Christ

Published by Calvary Chapel Publishing (CCP),
a resource ministry of Calvary Chapel of Costa Mesa
3800 Fairview Road
Santa Ana, CA 92704

Layout and Cover Design: Don Clark

Cover Photography: Kris McCaddon

First printing, 2002

ISBN: 1-9316-6713-6

Printed in the United States of America.

Dedication and Acknowledgements

I have so very much to thank God for when I think of the wealth of love He has shown me. I dedicate this book to my matchless Redeemer, Jesus Christ, to Whom I owe every good thing in my life.

I also give thanks for my dear wife Cathy; my cherished children: Jordan, Amy, Riley, and Nick; my loving mother Betty; and my brother and best friend, Kelley.

And a special thank you to those who helped me with this book: Robert and Linda Hayes, Elizabeth Griffin, Cathy Herholdt, and Jan Nelson.

Many Thousand Thanks,

Wayne Taylor

Introduction

The Apostle Paul tells us of his special mission from God in Ephesians 3:8, "*...that I should preach among the Gentiles the unsearchable riches of Christ.*" Paul's wonderful phrase, *the unsearchable riches of Christ,* is the topic of this book; and as we study Ephesians Chapter 1, we will discover many of those unsearchable riches.

The word unsearchable is fascinating because it means "un-trackable." You cannot track or keep track of the riches of Christ. They are too vast; they are too limitless; they are unfathomable and infinite. Of course, Paul is speaking of the spiritual riches that we have in Jesus Christ. We read in Ephesians 1:3, "*Blessed be the God and Father of our Lord Jesus Christ, who has blessed us with every spiritual blessing in the heavenly places in Christ.*" These blessings are the true riches, and there are so many. God's love is so vast, it will take forever to fathom.

By way of comparison, let's consider the riches of Microsoft founder Bill Gates who was once declared by *Forbes Magazine* to be the richest man on earth. His riches are hard to keep track of because they are changing so fast. At one point, he was declared to be worth 55 billion dollars. Can you imagine that much money? That is 13 billion more dollars than all the gold in Fort Knox. He has more money than 149 of the 191 countries of the world. Just 42 countries have more money than Bill. He could personally erase our country's entire federal deficit. If he were to purchase every professional baseball, basketball, football, and hockey team in North America, he would still have plenty of money to spare.

If you were to reduce Bill's 55 billion dollars to one-dollar bills and stack them up, they would stack 3,708 miles high. The stack would weigh over 11 million pounds, or 140 times more than a Boeing 747.

Let's say Bill wanted to spend all his money himself within the next few years. He would have to spend more than 12.5 million dollars **a day** for over 11 years!

Yes, Bill Gates is rich materially. Yet, as we see, his riches are not unsearchable. They are not un-trackable because we just tracked them. It may have been in strange ways, but we did it. However, his riches are nothing compared to the riches of Christ. God's riches are unsearchable. Our heavenly Father's pockets are bottomless. You can't measure the riches of Christ because they are infinite and they are eternal. Silver and gold are perishable and corruptible, but the riches of Christ are incorruptible. And we will be enjoying them forever and ever throughout eternity.

This book will give us the advantage of looking at some of those riches and at the effect that receiving Christ's riches should have upon our lives. We will look at a whole section dedicated to the riches we have in Jesus Christ; how we have been accepted, adopted, and become heirs; how we have received redemption and hope—the list goes on and on. As we learn of what is ours in Christ, we will be assured and empowered in our battle with Satan, the enemy of our souls.

Several years ago, we had a neighborhood bully who was harassing and threatening our children. The kids were fed up and ran to get me. I, of course, walked over with them to the play area. Oh, how empowered they suddenly felt—they were giddy with confidence. All their fear was gone as their adversary slunk away like a scared weasel.

As we receive in faith these wonderful riches of Christ, how should it affect us? Consider what Paul says in Ephesians 3:8, "*To me, who am less than the least of all the saints, this grace was given, that I should preach among the Gentiles the unsearchable riches of Christ.*" The vast love of Christ humbles me. I realize I don't deserve it, but Jesus is so good. He is so merciful to me and so kind. When I truly receive God's mercy and grace, the effect is that of Paul's response—I must tell others!

There are a whole lot of areas of our lives which need His mercy and grace. And the more you receive, the more you'll say, "I can't believe You still love me and that You're so good to me." When you receive His goodness, it puts a compulsion in your heart to tell others about Jesus. You'll want to share those wondrous riches, pass them on, and give your testimony of how good God has been to you. It's as Paul said, "Woe is me if I do not preach the good news!" (See 1 Corinthians 9:16.)

I personally have been so blessed to feast on these delicious helpings of God's banquet in Christ. I have been so nourished and strengthened spiritually. My desire for you as you read is that you will "*taste and see that the Lord is good*" (Psalm 34:8).

Day One
Opening the Treasure Chest

> *Paul, an apostle of Jesus Christ by the will of God, to the saints who are in Ephesus, and faithful in Christ Jesus: Grace to you and peace from God our Father and the Lord Jesus Christ. Blessed be the God and Father of our Lord Jesus Christ, who has blessed us with every spiritual blessing in the heavenly places in Christ.*
>
> *Ephesians 1:1-3*

I have always been a lousy fisherman. I like to fish, but I never catch any because fish hate me. Once, an expert fisherman wanted to take me out and show me how to do it. We went to a fishing hole where catching fish is guaranteed; and sure enough, he caught several. He even went so far as to get a fish on his line, and then he gave me the pole. Somehow, the fish knew who was holding the line and got away.

Several years ago, I decided I was going to catch a fish. I wanted to show my sons what it's like to go fishing and catch something, so we went to a fish farm. These streams were so packed with fish it was like throwing a line into a sardine can. It was so crowded in there that fish were pleading to be caught. So we did; we caught one fish after another to our hearts' content.

I believe this study in Ephesians Chapter 1 is going to be like that for many of you who have been struggling as Christians. Maybe you feel like you're a lousy Christian. Or maybe you have sought help from others, the so-called professionals, in your life. What you need is to feed on the Word, our spiritual nourishment, to make you stronger. But spiritual nourishment is not up on the top shelf where you can't get it. It's down in the lower cupboard where even little ones can get a hold of it. It's like a fish farm of spiritual nourishment. Ephesians Chapter 1 is just packed with a wealth of spiritual riches that we can claim.

The theme verse of this entire book is Ephesians 1:3, "*Blessed be the God and Father of our Lord Jesus Christ, who has blessed us with every spiritual blessing in the heavenly places in Christ.*" God the Father has blessed you, the believer, with every spiritual blessing in Christ Jesus. In other words, in Christ Jesus you are rich. You may not know it, but you are rich among all people; rich in your position in Christ and rich in the possessions that God has provided for you from the wealth of His nature.

Obadiah 17 says, "...*The house of Jacob shall possess their possessions.*" This talks about a future time when the children of Israel will actually possess all the land God previously promised them hundreds of years ago. They haven't yet possessed their possessions, but one day they will. Today, as children of God, He wants you to possess your spiritual possessions. He wants you to lay claim to the possessions He has given you so that you can be secure in your walk with the Lord and fruitful in your relationship with Him.

Ephesians is to the New Testament what Joshua is to the Old Testament. Joshua is about God's people going into the Promised Land and taking it. Likewise, I want you to get your flag of faith out and your hiking shoes on, and then go into this land and claim it! You need to say, "That's for me! God has promised it, and it's my rightful inheritance." It's not a matter of being selfish. It's a matter of not being ripped off anymore in your spiritual walk by unbelief and by Satan. We are talking about spiritual blessings galore.

You need to know what belongs to you so you can walk with God and fight the good fight of faith. So often, well-meaning preachers exhort you to fulfill your responsibilities. But how can you fulfill them when you are ignorant of the riches and resources available to you? You find in the Bible that the Lord always tells you what He has done for you before He asks you to do something for Him. He says, "This is what I've done, and this is what I've made available to you." The heaviness of responsibility is not on you—it's on Him. That's why you can rest. That's why you can be strong in the Lord and the power of His might.

Paul didn't tell us to be strong in ourselves and the power of our might. Why? Because Jesus knows we are weak, and His power is perfected in our weakness (Ephesians 6:10 and 2 Corinthians 12:9). The Lord shows us in Ephesians Chapter 1 all the wonderful things that belong to us.

Ephesus was a very great, but very wicked city. It was the hub of the idolatrous goddess Diana—the goddess of sexual orgies. The temple of Diana had thousands of prostitutes called priestesses, whose "business" financed the worship. The temple of Diana in Ephesus was one of the seven wonders of the ancient world. It was the largest Greek temple ever built—418 feet by 239 feet—and it had 127 ornate columns. It contained a vast wealth of art and paintings. Ephesus was one of the most prominent cities in the Roman Empire, second only to Rome, and it was the capital of Asia Minor.

Today, Ephesus does not exist except in ruins, and yet, it is an incredible place to visit. I have been there myself, and it is one of the most amazing archeological sites in the entire world. Aside from Jerusalem and Rome, probably the greatest archeological remains you'll ever see are at Ephesus. It has been uncovered, restored, and put back together as it was in ancient times. You go through the streets and see the columns, the library, the coliseum, and the theatre. It's just tremendous.

It was to this group of believers living in the city of Ephesus that Paul wrote. As Paul writes this book, it's hard to believe that he was writing from prison where he was chained to a Roman guard. He was a prisoner for no other reason than his faith, his witness, and his zeal for the Lord Jesus Christ. Yet as he was chained and imprisoned, he writes, "*Blessed be the God and Father of our Lord Jesus Christ, who has blessed us with every spiritual blessing in the heavenly places in Christ.*" "How could he say that? How could he be in such dire circumstances and yet write a book that is the Mount Rainier in the Cascades of Scripture?" you might ask.

Paul's secret was found in his fellowship with Jesus Christ. Everywhere he went, in any and every circumstance, Jesus was real to Paul. Our fellowship with Jesus is not just there in the happy, prosperous times, but in the hard, perilous times. Not just at church, but on the job. Not just at Bible study, but at the bowling alley and at Nordstrom, at that construction site where everyone is cursing, in that stressful office, and in that difficult situation. The love of Jesus can fill you anywhere, at any time, and in every season. Paul's prayer for us in Ephesians 3:16-19 is, "*that He would grant you, according to the riches of His glory, to be strengthened with might through His Spirit in the inner man, that Christ may dwell in your hearts through faith; that you, being rooted and grounded in love, may be able to comprehend with all the saints what is the width and length and depth and height—to know the love of Christ which passes knowledge; that you may be filled with all the fullness of God.*" That is my prayer for you.

Day Two
Paul, Bearer of Gifts

Paul, an apostle of Jesus Christ by the will of God...

Ephesians 1:1

The very first word in Ephesians is Paul. He is the one who wrote this letter, but Paul wasn't his given name. He was given the name Saul, which was a very common name for Jewish boys, especially those from the tribe of Benjamin. The very first king of Israel came from the tribe of Benjamin. That first king, who was the most exalted and famous man from that tribe, was King Saul. And Paul was given that exalted name, Saul. That was a fitting name for Paul. For a long time he was exalted, even self-exalted.

Paul described himself to the Philippians as "*circumcised the eighth day, of the stock of Israel, of the tribe of Benjamin, a Hebrew of the Hebrews; concerning the law, a Pharisee; concerning zeal, persecuting the church; concerning the righteousness which is in the law, blameless*" (Philippians 3: 5-6). In other words, "I was the holiest man around." He was very proud of that, and proud of his stock. Then something happened—he met Jesus face to face (Acts 9). He met the true holiest Man around, and suddenly Paul's résumé changed from holiest man to chief sinner (1 Timothy 1:15). Meeting the Lord has a way of doing that.

When you really see Christ in His glory, you see how awesome He is, and you realize, "I am not worthy of such a love." You become broken, and you are humbled. On his way to Damascus, Paul was knocked down; and as he lay there on his back with light flashing around him, Jesus said, "*I am Jesus, whom you are persecuting*" (Acts 9:5). Paul was converted. He changed his name from Saul to another name. He took on the name Paul, which literally means "little one." No longer a big man, but a little man with a big God.

Paul calls himself an apostle of Jesus. Apostle means, "one sent on a mission," like a missionary or ambassador. It can be likened to the U.S. Secretary of State who is an ambassador to the nations. Their mission is to represent the United States of America with all the authority of the government behind them.

As Christians, we are ambassadors (2 Corinthians 5:20). Our mission is the cause of Christ. We represent Christ, and our authority is nothing less than the name, the presence, and the government of Jesus Christ. Wow, that's authority!

Paul had a very special ambassadorship. The New Testament apostles were the founders of the Christian church. These guys had amazing authority, even to the point of writing New Testament Scripture, the very words of God. There are no apostles of that magnitude or authority today. Our authority is the Word of God. We have no authority beyond the Word of God given to us by the early apostles. There are no apostles today for the simple reason that the foundation has already been laid. The foundation is the first part of a structure that is laid down. In the early church, the apostles were that foundation. As we see in Ephesians 2:20, "*...having been built on the foundation of the apostles and prophets, Jesus Christ Himself being the chief cornerstone.*"

According to Ephesians 1:1, Paul was an apostle "*by the will of God.*" In other words, he didn't make himself an apostle. People cannot make themselves ministers of God's Word; God must call and empower them. Jesus called Peter, James, John, and Andrew when He told them, "*Follow Me, and I will make you fishers of men*" (Matthew 4:19). He makes people what He wants them to be through spiritual gifts. This is something that God does, and He does it with ordinary people. That's exciting!

Being a minister of God's Word is not necessarily the most important calling there is. Then what is? Whatever God is calling you to do is the most important calling. One time a shoemaker was being introduced to a clergyman.

The clergyman said "Hello, I am Thomas Smith, the most reverend, by the will of God." The shoemaker said, "Well, it's really good to meet you. I'm Bill Jones, shoemaker by the will of God." The greatest treasure in life is to do God's will, to represent Him, and to honor Him.

What are you by the will of God? Paul was "*an apostle of Jesus Christ by the will of God.*" Whatever you are, be that to God's glory. Maybe you're a carpenter by the will of God. Perhaps you have a skill or a talent. Maybe you are an administrator by the will of God or a secretary or a garbage man (or should I say *disposal engineer*?). Whatever God has called you to do, do it for His glory.

Day Three
God's Blank Check to Us

...To the saints who are in Ephesus, and faithful in Christ Jesus: Grace to you and peace from God our Father and the Lord Jesus Christ.

Ephesians 1:1-2

One day I did something I would never recommend doing—I went window-shopping with my two boys at Toys "R" Us. I warn you, if you don't have money, don't go to Toys "R" Us with kids. I did, and sure enough, Riley saw a toy that he wanted to buy. I told him I didn't have any money, so he asked me if I had any checks. I said that I did, and he suggested I write one. (They learn young, you know.) I told Riley that it's not good to write a check if you don't have any money in the account. He assured me it was okay, and I should just do it! Our earthly bank accounts might be low, but our heavenly Father's bank account is never lacking in all the spiritual riches He has given us. And we can never overdraw! He gives us a blank check for all His spiritual blessings.

Paul addresses this letter, "*To the saints who are in Ephesus...*" The term "saints" does not refer to an elite group of especially righteous people who are christened saints because of their great purity or religiosity. The word saint simply means "sacred one." It is a contrast between who you are and who you were. The simple fact that you are a believer in Christ makes you a saint. As a child of God, you are set apart for God. That's what the word saint means, "set apart for God." In other words, you are sacred, not secular. Even out there on that job, you are sacred—you are for God. You belong to Him.

Paul also calls the Ephesians "*faithful in Christ Jesus,*" literally, "full of faith in Christ Jesus." These are simply believers who believe fully, not some special group of believers who are better than others. A person who believes fully in Christ can be faithful to Christ. By trusting the Lord, you can be faithful. Maybe you say, "I just can't live the Christian life." Jesus can help you if you fully believe that He will help you. Put your trust as fully in Him as you can.

Paul writes, "*Grace to you and peace from God our Father and the Lord Jesus Christ.*" Grace and peace were the two main greetings in the Mediterranean world. Grace was the Greek greeting *charis,* meaning "unconditional blessing." It was like saying, "Free love and mercy to you." Peace, another Greek greeting, *eirene,* was spiritual as well as physical, meaning "prosperity to you, tranquility, and security." Notice that grace comes first. You really can't have peace without God's grace in the deepest sense of the word. You won't know peace without His loving mercy and grace, because true peace is from God and from the Lord Jesus Christ. You can have awesome peace and a sense of well-being because you know your position in Jesus Christ.

Take note of the phrase, "*in Christ Jesus.*" This phrase, or one similar to it, is used in Ephesians 27 times. In the first chapter alone, it is used 14 times. "*In Christ Jesus*" tells us of our position, our dwelling, our relationship. We are in the Lord. That is the theme of this book. You are in the Lord, and He is the one who is full of all the treasures. It's like living in a bank vault! You are living in Christ as a fish lives in water.

When I was five-years-old, I got my first pet: a goldfish. We lived in a little apartment, and I couldn't have a dog or a cat, so my mom got me a goldfish. I used to stare at that goldfish. Goldie was its name. I loved it so much that I decided one day to pet it. I took it out and put it on the table. It was wriggling around, and I thought it was just excited because it enjoyed it so much. Soon Goldie quit wriggling. Goldie had died. It died because it can only live in water.

Without Christ, we are dead. He is our only source of spiritual life. Thankfully, we can have fellowship with Christ at all times because we are in Christ. Draw near and let His presence fill you. That's what He desires for you.

Day Four
How Rich We Are

> *Blessed be the God and Father of our Lord Jesus Christ, who has blessed us with every spiritual blessing in the heavenly places in Christ.*
>
> *Ephesians 1:3*

If Jesus Christ is your Lord, you are extremely blessed. You are blessed by God the Father with every spiritual blessing in Christ. You are the object of His spiritual favor and riches. When you were born again through faith in Jesus Christ, you were born rich, richer than the Rockefellers. They may have billions of dollars, but their riches are temporary. Our riches in Christ last forever, and they are to be spent throughout eternity.

This knowledge caused Paul to burst forth with praise to God for all He has done for us. Reflecting on God's blessings makes us true worshipers. Romans 8:17 says we are fellow heirs with Christ, "*and if children, then heirs—heirs of God and joint heirs with Christ...*" God has become our Father too. How incredibly rich we are in Christ! Do you realize this? Is this amazing fact real to you?

You are blessed by God. His Spirit is upon you and within you wherever you go. Jesus told His disciples, "*And I will pray the Father, and He will give you another Helper, that He may abide with you forever*" (John 14:16). The disciples felt blessed to have Jesus with them. Whenever they needed something, Jesus was right there. He's with us too; ready to help in any circumstance we're going through. How rich we are. Our job is to believe, receive, and rely on our spiritual riches.

A sad but true story involves a man named Stanley William Walker, who was the son of a wealthy British ship builder. Stanley moved to Chicago, removing himself from contact with his father and family. He fell on hard times and became a homeless alcoholic on Chicago's Skid Row, living on the streets and begging for wine money so he could remain drunk.

After a while, his father died and left Stanley millions of dollars in inheritance. The authorities tried to locate him, but couldn't find him. Then one day, years later, on a cold Chicago night, he was found in a doorway lying next to a cheap bottle of wine, frozen to death. What a tragic story. Stanley never realized his fortune because he never found out about it. He was an heir to millions, but he lived as a beggar drinking cheap wine on dirty streets.

Many children of God are also living as spiritual beggars, groveling in sin and discouragement, seeking pleasure from the cheap wine of this world, not knowing they are heirs with Christ. God wants to give them rich, vintage Holy Spirit wine, which comes from a life of encouragement and purpose in fellowship with Jesus Christ and His people. Our first step is to grab onto that fact and believe it with all our hearts.

Where is it? It is in the heavenly places in Christ. God wants us to lift our eyes from earthly circumstances and the material things of this world and look up to Jesus. God's riches are not found in worldly possessions. God can and does provide earthly things for us, but that's not what we're talking about here. The things of Christ that deeply satisfy are found in seeking first the kingdom of God (Matthew 6: 33), and in setting our minds on the things above, not on the things below (Colossians 3:2).

Everything He wants to give us comes through our relationship and fellowship with Jesus Christ. Make this relationship number one in your life. Make it central in every circumstance—your marriage, your finances, your job, your parenting—let Jesus be the center.

Imagine your life as a wheel. Jesus should be the hub; everything else is a spoke. If you make Him a spoke, your life will be out of balance, and you'll have a very bumpy ride. If you make Jesus supreme and central in your heart, you will have the ride of your life!

Day Five
Chosen for His Priceless Love

> *...Just as He chose us in Him before the foundation of the world, that we should be holy and without blame before Him in love...*
>
> Ephesians 1:4

We are about to begin one long, glorious description of our spiritual blessings in Christ. The first of these blessings is that we are chosen by God.

Maybe you are someone who knows the pain of rejection. Maybe you haven't had much experience with being chosen. God wants to forever change that.

I remember one time when I was a kid and our class went roller-skating. It came to the "partners only" time where the girls chose who they wanted to skate with and the boys lined up, waiting to be chosen. I thought I'd be chosen first (Casanova that I was). Unfortunately, that didn't happen. There I was, the last one to be chosen, standing all by myself, feeling rejected. Then I noticed the cutest girl in the class hadn't chosen anyone yet. She came and picked me! Of course, I was the only choice left, but I didn't think about that. I went from the agony of defeat to the thrill of victory.

Jesus has had His eye of love on you for a long time. He chose you before the foundation of the world. Jeremiah 31: 3 says, *"I have loved you with an everlasting love..."* That's more than your wife, your mom, or anyone. How do you know this is true? Because He has drawn you with love. John 6:44 says, *"No one can come to Me unless the Father who sent Me draws him..."*

We think that we chose Christ and that the reason we belong to Him is because we searched for God and finally found Him. It's like the man who said to a boy, "Son, have you found Christ yet?" The boy answered, "I didn't know He was lost." In John 15:16, Jesus tells us, "*You did not choose Me, but I chose you...*"

Even though God chose us, we need to choose Him as well. God's decision does not negate our freedom and responsibility to choose Him. God doesn't choose losers; He picks winners. A winner is the person who chooses Him. When we do, we find out that He chose us first. He chose you first!

Notice that God chose us for a purpose, to be holy and blameless in His sight (2 Peter 3:14). He did not choose us so we could keep living a life of selfishness and impurity. His design is that we would be totally dedicated to Him. It is love that motivates us to live a consecrated life. God loved us and chose us, and Christ gave His life to save us from sin. When we realize that, we love Him and feel privileged to be spiritually married to Him.

When my wife Cathy and I first met, I was like many men—I felt timid and insecure about women. Previously, I had been in a relationship that lasted five years with a girl who wasn't ever sure she loved me. But Cathy was so kind and considerate. She was very caring and loving from the first day, while I was hesitant. After a year, she came to me one day with much excitement to tell me that God had told her she was to marry me. I said I wouldn't know whom I was going to marry until I walked down the aisle—not quite the response she was hoping for!

Cathy continued to be loving and caring and eventually won my heart and total devotion through her love. That's the way it is with the love of Jesus Christ. When you understand that He chose you and that He loves you, the result is that you want to live a life devoted to Him.

Day Six
God's Predestined Treasure

> *...Having predestined us to adoption as sons by Jesus Christ to Himself, according to the good pleasure of His will...*
>
> *Ephesians 1:5*

My mom's yard has a big old walnut tree in it that has always produced plenty of walnuts. As a kid, I found it frustrating to shell the walnuts. First of all, they are covered with a black, slimy skin that's very unpleasant, and then the shell is incredibly hard. I would try to crack them open with my teeth, but I couldn't. You've all heard the saying, "a hard nut to crack." Walnuts must have inspired that. But even if you do crack one, getting the nut out is not easy because there are so many crevices. You can rarely get it out whole. I think I managed it twice in 20 years. So the walnuts would just be left to rot on the tree or on the ground.

Some squirrels lived up in the tree, and they weren't frustrated at all by these walnuts. They didn't mind peeling off the slimy skin or patiently chipping away with their teeth on that hard shell. They would be out there with the nuts, holding them, flipping them around, and gnawing on them. For their patience, they received the reward—the nut, even though it was a hard one to crack.

Some Scripture passages are like that. They are somewhat hard to understand to our natural mind, maybe even hard to accept, even if we do understand. Today's verse might be like that for some. It talks about predestination. This subject can be difficult to grasp and receive, but I think if we are like those squirrels, if we take it slow and chip away at it, getting to the inside to understand, we'll find there is so much there to feed upon and enjoy.

Ephesians 1 verses 5 and 6 say, "*...having predestined us to adoption as sons by Jesus Christ to Himself, according* *to the good pleasure of His will, to the praise of the glory of His grace, by which He has made us accepted in the Beloved.*" You are a son, not just a slave. You can enjoy a close love relationship with God when you are under His grace. You can receive all of the blessings and inheritance He is offering right now.

God predestined us for these blessings, which means He planned this for us beforehand as our destiny. Predestination in Scripture is always a positive action of God for believers. It's never given in Scripture as a negative action of God. He doesn't predestine people to be lost, or predestine people to go to hell. People are lost; people will go to hell, but God doesn't predestine them for that.

It says in 2 Peter 3:9, "*The Lord...is not willing that any should perish but that all should come to repentance.*" Everyone has a choice. God knows who will repent and receive Jesus Christ. Romans 8:29 says, "*For whom He foreknew, He also predestined to be conformed to the image of His Son, that He might be the firstborn among many brethren.*" In other words, God has plans for you. He has a destiny for you and me.

You will find through this whole passage of Ephesians that God has a plan; He has a will. When we built our church building, we had plans. We didn't just say, "Let's build a church. You get some wood, I'll get some nails, and we'll throw this thing together. It'll be great!" We didn't do that. We wanted something that *really* would be great, so we made plans.

We had an architect draw up blue prints detailing every aspect: the plumbing, lights, electrical, doors, walls; everything about it was drawn out. When I first looked at the drawings, I thought, "These are really cool!" But I couldn't envision it. I couldn't see past those drawings because I'm not an architect. I didn't say, "I know exactly how it's going to look." Instead, I thought, "That's artistic!" But I can see the finished product now, and it looks even better than the architect envisioned.

God predestined. He drew up a good plan for you. Jeremiah 29:11 says, "'*For I know the plans that I have for you,' declares the LORD, 'plans for welfare and not for calamity to give you a future and a hope*'" (NASB). This is God's plan.

If a person refuses God, they can make a mess of their life. But the believers who desire God's will need to submit to God's work in their lives. It's exciting to put yourself in the Lord's hands and watch His plan for your life unfold.

Day Seven
The Jewel of Adoption

...Having predestined us to adoption as sons by Jesus Christ to Himself, according to the good pleasure of His will...

Ephesians 1:5

When parents adopt children, versus having their own, they have an advantage. Birth parents don't really have a choice concerning their kids; they have to take what they get. They are the parents of their children whether they like it or not. But parents who adopt make the choice to do so. As believers in Christ, we have been adopted into God's family. God chose to adopt us, not because He had to, but because He wanted to, because He loves you. He looked at you and said, "I want this person as my child." That means every believer. Notice in Ephesians 1:5 that it is "*by Jesus Christ to Himself.*" He adopted you to bring you to Himself. He wanted you to be with Him. How gracious He is.

It says in Romans 8:15, "*For you did not receive the spirit of bondage again to fear, but you received the Spirit of adoption by whom we cry out, 'Abba, Father.'*" The word *abba* is an Aramaic word that refers to a very intimate, close, affectionate relationship with a father. It literally means, "papa" or "daddy." God wants us to be that close.

God brought us to Himself. In Ephesians 2:13, Paul says, "*But now in Christ Jesus you who once were far off have been brought near by the blood of Christ.*" If you are a believer in Christ, you are near to God. You may not feel near, you may not feel close, but you are.

The phrase "*adoption as sons*" literally means to be given the standing of an adult son. Why is it such a blessing to be given the position or standing of an adult son? Because only adult sons and daughters receive the privileges and benefits of sonship. If you have a little two-year-old, you are not going to let him stay up all night. You're not going to say, "Here are the keys to the family car. Go take a spin." You're not going to give him his inheritance; he's too young. In a sense, when you're young, even though you're an heir, you are almost like a servant in the house, always being told what to do.

Galatians 4:1 says, "*Now...the heir, as long as he is a child, does not differ at all from a slave, though he is master of all.*" Verses 3-7 of Galatians 4 go on:

> *Even so we, when we were children, were in bondage under the elements of the world. But when the fullness of the time had come, God sent forth His Son, born of a woman, born under the law, to redeem those who were under the law, that we might receive the adoption as sons. And because you are sons, God has sent forth the Spirit of His Son into your hearts, crying out, "Abba, Father!" Therefore you are no longer a slave but a son, and if a son, then an heir of God through Christ.*

You are not just a slave. You are not under some legalistic religious system. You have a close, loving relationship with God when you are under His grace. You can receive all of the blessings and inheritance that He is offering in Ephesians 1 right now. He wants you to receive and enjoy them as His riches to you.

God has a great and wonderful plan. He wants to unfold it to you as you trust and surrender to Him. You have been adopted. You are a child of God.

Day Eight
Precious Acceptance

> *...To the praise of the glory of His grace, by which He has made us accepted in the Beloved.*
>
> *Ephesians 1:6*

As adopted sons in Christ, we have wonderful, total acceptance. Acceptance is one of the most vital blessings that you can have in life. Everyone is looking for acceptance. We all want to feel like we belong, that we are affirmed, that we are approved. Without a sense of acceptance, a person is insecure, often discouraged and defeated.

For Christians, there are those who continually strive to be good enough. Their Christianity becomes performance-based. They mistakenly think, "I just hope I can get to a point where God accepts me." There is very little peace, joy, or love. I am sad to say that for many Christians, maybe even a majority, this is their experience. It's the kind of Christianity they think is spoken of in the Bible. It's not. God accepts you fully and forever in Jesus Christ. He gives you the gift of total, wonderful acceptance when you receive Jesus Christ.

You cannot earn it. You cannot work for it. You cannot become good enough. In fact, Romans 4:5 says, "*But to him who does not work but believes on Him who justifies the ungodly, his faith is accounted for righteousness...*" Isn't that something? The Lord does not justify godly or holy people because there aren't any. All of us are sinners. However, when we trust Christ, our faith is accounted as righteousness. It's written down on our account in heaven, "justified, righteous, right with God, completely accepted." That's mine forever! I am accepted in the Beloved.

The devil doesn't want you to be assured that you are accepted and beloved by God. He wants you to think God is displeased or even disgusted with you. He wants you to feel that you are a sorry excuse for a Christian and you might as well give it up. But that's a lie.

The truth is that you are one of His precious, special children into whom He wants to pour His love. He wants you to know, "You are okay because My Son has given you worth. My Son has made you clean." Wow! I am so thankful for that. When I know that and live it, it gives me this great desire to please God, and it empowers me to serve Him and be what He wants me to be.

When I coached my son's third-grade basketball team, those boys were so zealous for basketball. They loved it! At one point, we were in a tournament with six teams, and we made it to the final four. There were my guys in the semi-final game, and they knew this was for the tournament. We were going for the championship, and they tried so hard!

Unfortunately, they dribbled the ball off their feet and traveled with the basketball. They passed to people who weren't looking and hit them on the head. They let their man go right by them, and because they made a big mistake like that, they ran down the court (especially my son) while looking at me. They would make this big bad move, and they looked at me for disapproval.

As a coach, there have been times when I've been disapproving. But I have learned if you do that, then the boys start pressing hard and feeling terrible; they start making more costly mistakes, and then they start crying. I really hate that.

So my son looked at me and said, "You hate me, don't you Dad?"

I looked back at him and responded, "No, you're doing great! It's fantastic! You are trying so hard. That's awesome! Keep going man! Don't feel bad. It's no big deal!"

My son let out a "whew" of relief and then ran over and fouled somebody else...but he was trying, and he'd just been rejuvenated. He went out and shot one from 20 feet...swish!

Yes!

Now, after the third quarter, because of all our errors, we were behind by nine. And in the third grade, at the end of the third quarter, that's like being behind by 40 in a normal college game. I told them, "You guys are doing so great! We're going to win it this quarter. You guys just pull together. Don't feel bad at all. You are going to win! I know you are! You are going to pull it off!" And we won. Those guys went out there and whipped the other team.

The Lord is not condemning you. He is not saying, "you are such a rotten Christian, I feel like rubbing you into the ground like a cigarette butt." He's not saying that at all. In fact, Isaiah 42:3 says, "*...a smoldering wick he will not snuff out*" (NIV). Rather, He fans it into flame. He blows on it, and it starts brightening up. You see, He knows that we are going to fail. He doesn't want us focusing on ourselves but rather on what He has done and what He will do. It is a love relationship. He hasn't given us a spirit of slavery, but the spirit of adoption as sons and we cry out, "Daddy, Papa." He affirms us.

He affirms you. He supports me. He accepts us.

Day Nine
Release from the Poverty of Sin - Part 1

> *In Him we have redemption through His blood, the forgiveness of sins, according to the riches of His grace which He made to abound toward us in all wisdom and prudence...*
>
> *Ephesians 1:7-8*

My pastor, Chuck Smith, likes to take old automobiles and make them like new. He took a '65 Chevy Corvette that was a piece of junk, refurbished it, and then gave it to one of his grandsons. I hear he does this for each of his grandchildren when they become old enough to drive. In fact, whenever one of my kids turn 16, I always encourage them to start calling him "Grandpa Chuck."

Pastor Chuck will also take a piece of property that has been trashed and make it like new. A retreat center had been terribly neglected and wasted over the years. He bought it, renewed it, and it is now a vibrant retreat center for Christians, and one of the most lovely Bible College campuses in the western United States. You could say it was redeemed.

Many times we see people downtown who are staggering around, wasted by alcohol and drugs, and we think, "Oh boy, there is no hope for them." But if Jesus comes into their lives and gets a hold of them, He makes them beautiful, valuable, and useful again. That's redemption.

Redemption is one of God's blessings promised to us in Ephesians. It is one of the main themes of the Bible. The Greek word for redemption, *apolutrosis,* literally means "to pay a ransom for something in order to liberate it," or "to purchase by paying a ransom in order to set free." Two truths we see about redemption are that it's costly and it's liberating.

Our redemption was expensive to God. Peter told us in 1 Peter 1:18-19, "*...you were not redeemed with corruptible things, like silver or gold, from your aimless conduct...but with the precious blood of Christ, as of a lamb without blemish and without spot.*" We were redeemed by His precious, pure blood.

Some people talk about "cheap grace." Grace is free to us, but it was very expensive to God. We were not redeemed by perishable things. Silver and gold are valuable on earth because they are very rare. Yet, in the eternal perspective, the streets of heaven are paved with gold—it's like asphalt in heaven. But where do you find sinless, human blood? That was the cost needed to pay the ransom for our sins because the wages of sin is death and without the shedding of blood, there can be no remission (Romans 6:23 and Hebrews 9:22). It took the pure, sinless blood of Jesus to pay for our sin.

Our redemption was so costly because we had sold ourselves into slavery to sin, just as it says concerning Israel in 2 Kings 17:17, "*[They] sold themselves to do evil in the sight of the LORD, to provoke Him to anger.*" Jesus said, "*For what profit is it to a man if he gains the whole world, and loses his own soul?*" (Matthew 16:26). In other words, what will you give to gain all that you desire? What will you compromise? What values will you let go of to get what you want? We tend to cheapen our own lives by selling ourselves to the mastery of some selfish pursuit or sin.

Though this is true of all of us in one way or another, God values us highly. He purchased us with the powerful, cleansing blood of His Son. This blood is not only costly, but it has the power to release us from the bondage and slavery we were sold into—namely sin. In Romans 7:14, Paul tells us that God's law is spiritual but we are of flesh, sold into bondage to sin. Sinning did not make us sinners. Rather, because we were born sinners, we sin. We inherited a fallen nature, and we followed in the same footsteps of our father, Adam, who, for passing pleasure, chose sin. We are of flesh. That's why it's an impossible task to try to free ourselves from selfishness, sin, and the fallen human nature. Even as a Christian, I find it is impossible to try to liberate myself from the things that easily stumble me.

But there is a powerful element that God wants to give to me. It is the blood of Christ and the power of His presence, His Holy Spirit in my life. The one who sins, Jesus said, is the slave of sin (John 8:34). We were enslaved by sin's guilt and power, and sin is a very harsh master. But Jesus' blood releases us from both the guilt and the power of sin because in Him we have redemption through His blood, the forgiveness of sins.

The Greek word for forgiveness, *aphesis*, literally means "freedom." It refers to being loosed from that which binds a person. Jesus declares you the believer free from the sins that have enslaved you. He has opened wide the prison doors—don't stay in your cell. In faith, walk out with Christ into glorious liberty.

Day Ten
Release from the Poverty of Sin - Part 2

> *In Him we have redemption through His blood, the forgiveness of sins, according to the riches of His grace which He made to abound toward us in all wisdom and prudence...*
>
> Ephesians 1:7-8

Satan loves to keep us under guilt and a sense of failure and condemnation, even after we have confessed and repented, so he can keep us in that place of slavery to sin. He wants to keep us defeated, despairing, and giving in to sin, when the truth is we are liberated by Jesus, we are forgiven and washed white as snow (Isaiah 1:18). That is a fabulous gift to us from God, but the devil wants to keep us in condemnation because that way our hearts are kept impure and are still enslaved. The Apostle Paul says, "*...for all have sinned and fall short of the glory of God, being justified freely by His grace through the redemption that is in Christ Jesus, whom God set forth as a propitiation by His blood, through faith...*" (Romans 3:23-25).

What does that mean? Propitiation is a big religious word that is packed with meaning. Like redemption, propitiation is one of the most glorious words in the Bible. Propitiation means "a sacrifice that satisfies God's judgment against sin and releases His mercy." In other words, this sacrifice is so satisfying, it appeases all of God's wrath against our sin and releases all of God's mercy as a gift. That's propitiation. That is what Jesus is. His sacrifice was magnanimous, huge, and glorious!

The Apostle John said, "*If we confess our sins, He is faithful and just to forgive us our sins and to cleanse us from all unrighteousness*" (1 John 1:9). In other words, if you confess your sins and believe in Jesus for the forgiveness of them, God is only right to forgive you and cleanse you of every sin. Why? Because those sins have already been punished. Criminals don't have to pay twice for their crime; they just have to pay once. A double punishment is against the law. Jesus took our punishment. It wouldn't be right if God didn't forgive us if we believe in Jesus.

Because of this, I am forgiven, and my conscience is cleansed. That gives me freedom to realize that God made me for a greater purpose. He didn't make me to live for myself or to be a slave of an appetite or a desire. He made me to be a slave of my Maker who knows exactly what is best for me and how He wants to use me.

Ephesians 1:7 says that we have forgiveness of sins according to the riches of His grace, which Christ made to abound toward us in all wisdom and understanding. You see, what sin does is cloud our understanding; it brings confusion. You've probably noticed that, as a Christian, when you stumble and sin, you get caught in a cycle of defeat. You're almost like a zombie. Spiritually you go into this dust storm. It's like tornados that come and create havoc and death. Sin is like that with its consequences and guilt. It stirs up total confusion, and you lose your spiritual understanding. But when you receive forgiveness through the blood of Christ, His grace and mercy cleanses the guilt and confusion. It is like a beautiful gentle rain clearing the smog out of the air. You can see "God has something more for me. I'm not a scumbag. I am a child of God. I am a servant of God." He made His grace to abound toward us in all wisdom and understanding.

Romans 5:20 says, "*But where sin abounded, grace abounded much more.*" That Scripture makes me do cartwheels! How do you receive that abundance? Paul asked in Romans 6:1-2, "*Shall we continue in sin that grace may abound? Certainly not*!" If you take that line of thinking, you're saying that you are forgiven and cleansed so you can go back to the very thing that trapped and enslaved you, that brought confusion and damage to your heart as if sin was the greatest pleasure in the world. It's not great; it's garbage. Fulfilling desires outside the will of God is garbage.

Fulfilling desires and pleasures within God's will is really living. It's a joy.

We receive His grace, not to keep sinning, but so that we can be all He wants us to be. We can rise up to a higher plane of life. As Jesus said, "*Therefore if the Son makes you free, you shall be free indeed*" (John 8:36).

In Romans 6:16, we are told that we will be the slave of either sin leading to death, or the slave of God and righteousness leading to abundant life. How do we enter into that abundant life? First, we really need to believe that when we confess our sins and when we receive God's mercy and grace, it is ours and we are redeemed. We are valuable to God. We are highly esteemed. He will liberate us to a higher way of living. We need to believe that. We then need to yield to the Holy Spirit and become a slave to Him. Romans 15:13 says, "*Now may the God of hope fill you with all joy and peace in believing, that you may abound in hope by the power of the Holy Spirit.*"

The abundant life comes through really believing in His grace, which He made to abound to us, and then yielding to the Spirit. In John 10:10, Jesus tells us the thief, the devil, has come to steal, kill, and destroy. Satan wants to rip you off of God's best for your life every single solitary day by throwing temptations at you that will steal, spoil, and enslave your life. That is the way it is with sin. It's like Lay's potato chips. "You can't eat just one." Sin is progressive like that. It robs you and deadens you spiritually. Jesus concludes John 10:10 by saying, "*I have come that they may have life, and that they may have it more abundantly.*" This comes through God's abundant grace and the gift of His Holy Spirit.

The word abundant is a great word. It means, "wave upon wave, endlessly, continuously." Have you ever sat on an ocean beach and watched the waves breaking? They just keep coming in. You wonder, "Where are those coming from?" Well, there is a great big ocean out there! So it is with

God's grace. There is an ocean. It is infinite, exemplified in the gift of Christ. And there are waves and waves of grace for your life. There are some soft gentle waves. There are some thrilling waves He wants you to catch. And yes, there are some hard breaking waves. But they are all meant to give you more of Christ, more of His power and His love in our lives. That is the abundant life.

Day Eleven
God's Platinum Purpose - Part 1

> *...Having made known to us the mystery of His will, according to His good pleasure...*
>
> *Ephesians 1:9*

I was reminded of something I used to do with my dad when I was a kid when my youngest son Nick came up to me and said, "Dad, let me walk on your feet." He put one foot on one of my feet, one on the other, then took my hands, and we walked together through the house. At first, he was facing toward me and couldn't see where we were going. He was a little nervous, but he trusted me, especially since I didn't ram him into any tables or chairs. Then he turned around, and we started walking with him facing out but still on my feet. This time he could see where we were going. It was great fun. I remember when I did this with my dad, I used to like to stomp on his feet, but my son is much nicer than that.

After a while, Nick wanted to lead. He couldn't lead with me on his feet, so he wanted to lead from the top position. As you can guess, it didn't work very well because he wasn't carrying me. We ended up getting kind of off track and ran into a wall.

The Lord wants us to put our feet on His. He wants us to take His hand and let Him lead us in His ways. He has a will and a purpose for our lives. Sometimes you can see Him working. It's as if you are looking right into His eyes as you see things happen and think to yourself, "Wow, the Lord is really at work." Other times, you can't see it as clearly. You see things happening and you ask, "Where is God in this?" But the Lord wants you all along to believe in Him and to submit to His will. He doesn't want us to tell Him what to do, but to ask Him what His will is. That's what prayer is—searching out His wonderful will.

Notice in Ephesians 1:9, the words refer to His purpose, His will, His pleasure. He wants your life to be full of meaning and the full purpose of His will. Sadly, we live in an age in which most people don't believe in divine purpose for the world or for their lives.

A man named Andre Maurois summed up the modern view of the world when he said, "The universe is indifferent. Who created it? Why are we here on this puny mud heap spinning in infinite space? I have not the slightest idea. And I am quite convinced that no one has the least idea."[1]

It is no wonder that people of our generation and of the last century have fallen into such a sad philosophy. We are reaping the pitiful fruit of the belief in evolution. If you believe that we evolved by random chance from the primordial slime, then life has no sense of meaning. You are not the purposeful creation of a loving God. You are just a slime ball (advanced of course).

We have been robbed of divine purpose, meaning, and hope. Without hope or without divine purpose there is a void. Rushing to fill the void is a false and selfish purpose. The motto is "survival of the fittest." That is the way people live, rather than loving God and others the way Christ has said.

Regardless of whether people believe that there is a divine purpose, or whether they are submitted to God or not, His will is going to prevail in the end. Even those who refuse Him and rebel against Him will fulfill His purpose, although it will be His plan of judgment against rebellion, not the loving, joyous purpose He wants each and every one of us to fulfill.

Day Twelve
God's Platinum Purpose - Part 2

> *...That in the dispensation of the fullness of the times He might gather together in one all things in Christ, both which are in heaven and which are on earth--in Him. In Him also we have obtained an inheritance, being predestined according to the purpose of Him who works all things according to the counsel of His will...*
>
> *Ephesians 1:10-11*

Everything is headed towards the reality that one day every knee will bow and every tongue will confess that Jesus Christ is Lord to the glory of God the Father (Philippians 2:10-11). We all have the choice to either bow voluntarily with an open heart, saying, "I need the Savior that You have given me," and be a wonderful part of His will, or to bow later by force and perish. God's purposes will be accomplished. He is God.

In Ephesians 1:10, dispensation is translated from the Greek *oikonomia,* meaning "the administration of the household." It is the source of the English word "economy." The economy of God is not speaking of money. The economy of God is about how He is administrating, how He is directing, and what is really going to last. One day, we will give an account of ourselves, and we'll want to be part of His economy, of His administration, part of serving within His kingdom. Christ is going to execute His Lordship over all one day, including this rebellious planet. Both in heaven and on earth, anything that is going to last will have to be in Christ. Everything outside of Christ will perish.

You are not a random accident of evolution. You are an act of God. He was active in planning and making you, and Christ has redeemed you for a reason. You have a purpose to your life. He loves you and wants you to follow God's will.

Jesus planned for you to be here. He planned for you to follow Him. The word "will" in Ephesians 1:11 is interesting.

It is not the Greek word *boulema,* for "desire based on reason," but it is the Greek word *thelema,* for "desire based on emotion." In other words, God is not just an infinite mind. He does have an infinite mind; He is infinitely intelligent, but He also has an infinite heart of love. That heart of love has determined to plan a will, a meaning, and a purpose for you.

Whereas His will was in the past a mystery, now He has made it known to believers in Christ. He wants you to know it. To some believers, it is still a mystery, and they would like to keep it that way so they won't have to do it. But we misunderstand because God's will is not some negative thing. He's not going to make me do something I hate. He won't make me marry someone I don't like, or send me to some far off tribe just to make my life miserable.

God, our heavenly Father, is very loving. As a father, I love to lead my children toward things they enjoy. Yes, there are some things that I need to help them learn to enjoy, but that's the point. "*For it is God who works in you both to will and to do for His good pleasure*" (Philippians 2:13).

God is not dumb. It's very difficult to get people motivated to do the things they hate. So the Bible says in Psalm 37: 4, "*Delight yourself also in the LORD, and* ***He shall give you*** *the desires of your heart* (emphasis mine)." God says, "Take pleasure in Me, enjoy Me, and I will satisfy the very desires of your heart. Those desires that you have will actually become My will for you." God is very smart. He puts His own desires in your heart when you are delighting yourself in Him.

This verse doesn't mean that He plans to fulfill every desire you've ever had, even the wicked ones, because that would hurt you. I believe He wants to fulfill every aspect of your life, but not in an evil way. He wants to fulfill you in the best way, His way. Trust Him because "Father knows best." His ways are higher than our ways, like the heavens are higher than the earth (Isaiah 55:9). Following Jesus gives us ultimate purpose and pleasure.

Day Thirteen
God's Platinum Purpose - Part 3

> *...That...He might gather together in one all things in Christ...that we who first trusted in Christ should be to the praise of His glory...*
>
> *Ephesians 1:10, 12*

This is God's purpose for our lives, in a general sense, "*that we who first trusted in Christ should be to the praise of His glory.*" This is true of everyone, whether the first ones saved or the last ones saved. If we have trusted in Christ, we should be to the praise of His glory. That is why you and I are here, that we might live to the praise of His glory. The Greek word for praise, *epainos*, literally means, "commenting on a story."

When we tell stories about our life, we tend to tell them in a way that puts us in an exalted light. When I tell my story, I am the knight in shining armor. Or sometimes I will tell it in a negative way, putting myself down if it is funny. But if it's not a funny story, I am going to make sure I look good. God wants the story of our life to put Christ in an exalted light, not ourselves. That's praise.

The story of our life exalts Christ because we were created for the praise of *His glory*, not for the praise of our glory. Living for ones own glory results in a very shallow and superficial life. Yet, that seems to be the modern trend.

Watch the Oscars. The actors may be entertaining the masses, but they are in the business for the praise of Hollywood's glory. It says in Proverbs 25:27, "*It is not good to eat much honey; so to seek one's own glory is not glory.*" It is not good for you to eat too many sweets, nor is it good to sit around and think of your own glory or seek your own glory. You are to seek to let your life glorify God.

What if you had tremendous talent, like some of these famous actors and singers, but you spent your whole life just glorifying yourself? This is what most people are doing or seeking to do. God has so much more. He wants your life to have meaning.

Paul asked the question in 1 Corinthians 4:7, "... *And what do you have that you did not receive? Now if you did indeed receive it, why do you boast as if you had not received it?*" In other words, God has given you everything you have. You could say, "I have so much talent," or, "I am so beautiful." But you didn't make yourself. You didn't give yourself aptitudes, abilities, and skills. God did. Therefore, our Creator is the one who is to be glorified. God wants us to use our talents to share Christ.

God's purpose is to gather everyone together into the ark of Christ, just like in the Old Testament, during the flood. Noah had an ark. He was to gather all the animals and as many people who would go in as possible. God wants to use us to help gather people into the ark because everything else is going down. Christ is our ark.

We read in the story of Noah that he didn't have to go into the far reaches of the jungle to gather the animals. God brought the animals to him. Likewise, witnessing and being a light is not a gigantic chore. The Lord brings people across our path every day that we might gather them in. God just wants us to be open and point them to Himself. You may think that they are not interested at all, but they are! They would love to know God. They just need to see that He is real in someone who knows Him. If you tell them your story, they are drawn in. Not everyone is going to believe, but many will.

Drawing others to Christ is a wonderful experience, and it is part of the purpose of our life. In the end, only those who come into the safe haven of Christ are going to remain. Anyone outside of Christ is going to perish because sin has separated us from God and torn this world apart. Sin has torn us up inside and torn us apart from one another. Sadly, sin has ripped us away from God, but Christ is gathering people back and uniting them to Himself.

Regrettably, we live in a world that is so fractured and fragmented, full of strife and division: division between black and white, young and old, women and men, rich and poor, liberals and conservatives. But the division is much deeper than that. We have been torn from our Maker by sin, but Jesus Christ was broken on the cross. His body was torn so that I could be made whole and restored to God. Then I can be joined with other people who are restored to God, and become part of the body of Christ that is being gathered together.

Now, as I am restored to God and made whole, my life can glorify Jesus. That is why I am here. As I have joined with you and we are gathered into one, then together as a body we can glorify Jesus. That is why we are here. That is the purpose and that is the meaning.

God says, "I am making this beautiful tapestry of your life." When we look at our lives, all we see are loose ends, but we are looking at the back of the tapestry. We don't see all that He is doing. From God's heavenly viewpoint, He sees the image of Christ. The glory of Christ is being shown. Your life may look like a mess, but God is working. He wants you to trust Him.

Each day he wants you to cooperate with Him, to obey what His Word says, and to try to live for His glory. As you do, that glory of Christ, that likeness of Christ, together with the rest of us, will become evident and shown.

I once saw a collage of all the names of the states in the United States of America. Each state name was printed in a different and beautiful font, and then woven together into a picture that formed the face of George Washington, the father and first president of our country. Each of us, as children of God, has been uniquely and beautifully made by our heavenly Father. Our greatest glory is to unite together in expressing and magnifying Him.

Day Fourteen
A Rich Inheritance

...In whom also we have obtained an inheritance, being predestined according to the purpose of Him who works all things according to the counsel of His will...

Ephesians 1:11

I am not one to believe in getting rich quick or getting something for nothing. In fact, when commercials for a sweepstakes come on trying to get me to sign up for a drawing, I never do. Ed McMahon doesn't really inspire me. They show his truck driving up and a person getting this huge check, and I always wonder what bank is going to cash a 10-foot check. It's way too big! But the thing that does inspire me is the expression of amazement and the thrill in the eyes of the people who win. All of a sudden, they are millionaires. I know that feeling, not because I have ever won anything like that, but because of the incredible treasure that Christ has bestowed on me. I am so amazed that He laid aside this inheritance for me!

God has drawn up the richest Will that has ever been written. He made it out to His heirs, and I am one of the beneficiaries (Hebrews 9:15). And if you are a believer in Christ, you are a beneficiary too. A Will is not applied or executed until the person who made the Will dies. That is one of the reasons why Jesus died, so that you and I could become heirs with Him of the riches of God. He also rose again so He could make sure that we get our portion of the inheritance.

What has God given to Jesus Christ as His inheritance? The Father has given Him all things in the universe. In John 3:35, Jesus says, "*The Father loves the Son, and has given all things into His hand.*" Hebrews 1:2 says that God appointed Jesus "*heir of all things.*" What's amazing is that if you are a child of God, the Bible says His Spirit, the Holy Spirit, bears witness with your spirit that you indeed are a child of God, and if a child of God, an heir of God and a joint heir with Jesus Christ (Romans 8:16-17). Think of that! We are fellow heirs with Jesus, if we suffer with Him, that we may also be glorified with Him.

Paul goes on to say in Romans 8:32, "*He who did not spare His own Son, but delivered Him up for us all, how shall He not with Him also freely give us all things?*" One day we will be inheriting the universe with our husband, Jesus Christ. Talk about marrying into wealth! Being part of the bride of Christ is an awesome thing. No wonder Jesus said in Luke 12:32, "*Do not fear, little flock, for it is your Father's good pleasure to give you the kingdom.*" What a day that will be!

One day as the disciples were walking along, Peter was thinking to himself that they had really given up a lot for Jesus. They had sacrificed homes and relatives, possessions and careers. But Jesus replied, "*...There is no one who has left house or brothers or sisters or father or mother or wife or children or lands, for My sake and the gospel's, who shall not receive a hundredfold now in this time—houses and brothers and sisters and mothers and children and lands, with persecutions—and in the age to come, eternal life*" (Mark 10:29-30). Since becoming a Christian, look how big your family has become; it's thousands of times bigger than it was before. "*...And in the age to come, eternal life*" with God—Christ gives us that awesome inheritance!

The Lord doesn't just have heaven for you in the next life. He has heavenly places for you in this life. In other words, close intimate fellowship with Him and blessings galore are here for you. We see some of those blessings in 1 Corinthians 3:21-23 where it says, "*Therefore let no one boast in men. For all things are yours: whether Paul or Apollos or Cephas, or the world or life or death, or things present or things to come—all are yours. And you are Christ's, and Christ is God's.*" Notice Paul is saying we belong to Him and to each other. But He also says all things are yours as a child of God. He owns everything, and He has given everything to us to enjoy.

That doesn't mean you actually own everything right now. You can't go out in the parking lot and take your choice of cars thinking, "The Bible says it all belongs to me." Nonetheless, there is much that you are able to enjoy right now, like all the people He has blessed you with and beautiful places you can get pleasure from without owning. It's a little bit like being a grandparent. You don't necessarily have to raise the children, but you can have fun with them.

In this life, the Lord has blessed us with so much. Think of Abraham. God told Abraham He would give him the Promised Land. When Abraham went there, he took Lot along. As they worked the land, they each began to prosper. Their shepherds had huge flocks, and they started encroaching upon each other's land. Abraham's and Lot's men began fighting and arguing, until Abraham stepped in and said, "Hey, let's not fight, we are brothers. I tell you what, Lot, you take whatever land you want. You have first choice. I give it all to you."

Abraham was completely unselfish. On the other hand, Lot became very selfish, and he took the best part. He said, "Oh, I can have anything? I just want the best part." It's sad because Lot more or less lived for himself and for the pleasures of Sodom and Gomorrah. Yet, what happened? He ended up losing everything. What a lesson. Jesus said, "*Do not lay up for yourselves treasures on earth, where moth and rust destroy and where thieves break in and steal; but lay up for yourselves treasures in heaven...*" (Matthew 6:19-20).

Even if you are blessed materially on this earth, use it to invest in the things that are going to last. Abraham was a man who was extremely blessed materially. He had a lot of wealth. Even after Lot made his choice and took the best, the Lord appeared to Abraham and said, "That was nice of you to do that for Lot, but I want to tell you something. I want you to come up here on this hill, and I want you to look as far north as you can, as far east, as far west, and as far south. All the way to the horizon is yours—the whole thing! I am even giving you what Lot chose" (Genesis 13:14-17).

It is interesting that even though God blessed Abraham materially, he always saw himself as a pilgrim, traveling light. In fact, in Hebrews 11:8-10, we learn that he was looking for a better country, a lasting one, whose builder and maker was God. He was looking for a heavenly city. Actually, Abraham only owned the deed to one piece of property while he lived on this earth—his own gravesite. He understood that all of this is going to pass away, but what's really going to last is investing in God's kingdom that will come. That touched the heart of God. It says in Genesis 15:1, "*Do not be afraid, Abram. I am your shield, your exceedingly great reward.*" In other words, "I've got an inheritance for you; it's Me." Jesus is saying to us, "I am yours, and all that I own belongs to you."

Day Fifteen
Sharing the Wealth

> *In Him you also trusted, after you heard the word of truth, the gospel of your salvation...*
>
> *Ephesians 1:13*

The message of salvation through Jesus Christ has been spread to millions of people for the last 2,000 years by one believer telling someone else the good news. God wants to use you and me as reporters of His message. He wants us to be heralds of the gospel so that everyone can know the truth. The Bible says in Romans 10:15, "*As it is written: How beautiful are the feet of those who preach the gospel of peace, who bring glad tidings of good things!*" God Himself is actually praising the feet of those who bring the good news to their neighbors. Normally, feet are not the part of your body that people praise. They are probably the least attractive part of your body. You seldom hear that you have beautiful feet or handsome toes. Even beautiful people can have ugly feet. But God is saying we can have beautiful feet.

I could kiss the feet of the guy who brought me the good news. I love his feet because he went out of his way to tell me about Jesus, to bring Christ to me. Man, I am so thankful for that guy! His feet are beautiful to me, but more importantly, they are beautiful to God.

How beautiful are your feet to the Lord? When we get to heaven, if you have sought to be a witness, people are going to come up to you and kiss your feet! They will be so thankful that you didn't keep it to yourself, that you told them. Your feet can be lovely to the Lord.

Ephesians 1:13 tells us that hearing God's Word incites faith in people. The Bible also says, "*...Faith comes by hearing, and hearing by the word of God*" (Romans 10: 17). God uses His word to stir the hearts of people and the result is belief in Christ and growth in faith. It's the Word of

God, God's powerful message shared, that arouses faith in people.

Often people ask me how they can get a friend, brother, or cousin to believe. Well, you can't, but God can. Belief can happen when you present them with the message of the gospel or tell them the truth of God's Word, the Scripture. Isaiah 55:11 says His Word will not return void without accomplishing the purpose for which He sent it. God didn't say that about my words. My words have returned void many times. They can ring very empty. But His Word will not return void. Just as rain comes down from heaven and waters the earth, causing life to bud, blossom, and bring forth fruit, even so it is when God's Word is shared. It doesn't return empty. It will accomplish, He says, what He sent it for, and it will prosper.

Now you don't have to necessarily quote chapter and verse or use the King James translation when you are talking to people about the message. You can say it in your own words, and it will pierce like a sharp sword, stirring faith in those who hear (Hebrews 4:12).

It is also true that hearing God's Word is what really makes your faith strong. Many people have said to me, "I am just really weak in faith." Well, I have the answer. According to Romans 10:17, faith comes by hearing the Word of God. Feed upon the Word of God, and your faith will grow. If you base your faith on your feelings from day to day, you are going to have a very weak faith. Many Christians do that because, as people, we are so feelings-oriented. And chances are, we transpose that onto how God feels about us. It's not so. God is not in a bad mood. He is not angry with you. He hasn't changed. He loves you as much as He ever has. His mercies are "*new every morning*" (Lamentations 3:23). That is what His Word says. My faith is based upon His promises, His Word, His truth. I would be so up and down if it weren't for the nourishing Word.

Sharing the Wealth

The more you take in the Word, the more you want. Sometimes people tell me that my children have really grown, and I say that they do grow if I feed them. That's kind of a joke, but it's true. You feed them, they grow, and as they grow, you have to feed them more because they get hungrier and hungrier as they get older. That's why your food bill keeps going up.

It's like that with God's Word. If you cultivate your appetite, it shows that you're alive because you're hungry, and the more you take in, the hungrier you get. That is how you grow. If you are not cultivating that appetite, you are not growing the way God wants you to grow. He loves you. He wants you to be strong in faith, so feast on His Word and share it with others so they will grow too.

Day Sixteen
His Sealed Purchase

> *...In whom also, having believed, you were sealed with the Holy Spirit of promise, who is the guarantee of our inheritance until the redemption of the purchased possession, to the praise of His glory.*
>
> *Ephesians 1:13-14*

What does it mean to be sealed with the Holy Spirit of promise? Well, the Greek word for sealed, *sphragizo*, literally means, "to be stamped with a special mark," or in this case, to be stamped with God's mark. And that means several wonderful things, four of which we will look at today.

First, it is a mark of ownership. You are sealed with the Holy Spirit. That means you belong to God. People often put a mark of ownership, like their signature, on something they own. This means, "I own it, so don't take it." It's like my Bible in which I've written my name. If you find it, don't take it. It belongs to me. I paid nine dollars for it—I am so cheap, you can't believe it. You'd think a pastor would have more than a nine-dollar Bible, but I like it. It is so simple. Yes, the cover is made out of cardboard, but who cares? It belongs to me.

The Lord paid a lot more than nine dollars for you and me. "*Or do you not know that your body is the temple of the Holy Spirit who is in you, whom you have from God, and you are not your own? For you were bought at a price...*" (1 Corinthians 6:19-20). What is that price? It's the precious blood of Jesus Christ. Therefore glorify God in your body and in your spirit, which are the Lord's. God has given us the Holy Spirit to let us know that we belong to Him. The Holy Spirit is His signature upon you. You belong to God.

As it says in Romans 8:9, "*But you are not in the flesh but in the Spirit, if indeed the Spirit of God dwells in you. Now if anyone does not have the Spirit of Christ, he is not His.*" You see, God gave you the Holy Spirit. You belong to Him. You're not in the flesh. You are not to be dominated by selfishness. He has given you the Spirit of Christ. You are in the Spirit; you belong to Christ. Praise the Lord! The Holy Spirit is God's mark of ownership on us.

Secondly, to be stamped with God's mark means the sealing of the Holy Spirit. It is a mark of security. He has put His seal upon you, and He knows those who belong to Him. A Roman seal was placed upon the tomb of Jesus to keep it secure and undisturbed and to keep Jesus from rising from the dead (Matthew 27:66). Now that was a pretty ridiculous thing to do; nevertheless, Caesar's seal was put upon the tomb as he had asked to make it as secure as possible.

No human seal could ever withstand God and His will. When God puts His seal upon something, it is as secure as anything could ever be. Because His seal is on it, it cannot be ripped off. It cannot be disturbed. He guarantees His security, His protection. He sealed us with the Holy Spirit of promise. Paul tells us in Ephesians 4:30, "*And do not grieve the Holy Spirit of God, by whom you were sealed for the day of redemption.*" The Holy Spirit is God's pledge that He will take us through to that day of redemption. You are sealed and secured.

Thirdly, the sealing of the Holy Spirit is a mark of identification and genuineness. The actual Greek word for sealed is literally "stamped," and it refers to stamping or branding an object with an impression or image. It's not like a postage stamp, but like an embossing stamp used to impress an image in wax. God gives us the Holy Spirit to stamp upon us His image, the image of Christ. That is His stamp, His brand. So our hearts need to be softened like wax before the Lord so that the impression of Christ can be made on us. The Holy Spirit is branding the likeness of Jesus on us. That is a sign that we are genuine. It is a testimony to ourselves that we have the Holy Spirit. Christ is being formed in us. The Holy Spirit is in us, marking us with His image as the genuine article, a true believer.

This branding can hurt sometimes. I think of branding cattle, as my grandfather used to do. He was a rancher, and I would watch him brand his horses and cattle. When he would brand a cow, its hide would sizzle, and even those big, strong cows would flinch. Of course, it was painful. In the same way, it is painful to us as the Holy Spirit burns our flesh away so that the likeness of Christ can stand out. It hurts, but it is a good pain. If there are painful things happening in your life, God is doing a work. He wants to burn away that selfishness so the beauty of Christ can shine out. It is a mark of identification, the likeness of Christ, and it shows that we are genuine.

Finally, the sealing of the Holy Spirit means preservation and guaranteed delivery. The Holy Spirit preserves and delivers all the way. As Ephesians 1:14 says, the Holy Spirit *"is the guarantee of our inheritance until the redemption of the purchased possession."* One time, I went to the post office and sent a package marked "Special Delivery" to my friend in Oregon. It cost a little bit more, but I wanted to make sure it would get there. My friend called to tell me he received the package. It had been handled with care all the way there because it had that mark of "Special Delivery" on it.

You have that special mark of the Holy Spirit. You are a special delivery that God is bringing all the way to heaven. Christ not only saved you previously, He is going to keep you saved presently. How? It's through the Holy Spirit within you. Without the Holy Spirit, we would never make it! But God has given us the Holy Spirit to take us all the way. And Christ says of us, as He prayed for His disciples in John 17: 12, *"[Father]...I kept them in Your name. Those whom You gave Me I have kept; and none of them is lost..."* He is not going to lose you.

The Holy Spirit is a mark of ownership, security, identity, genuineness, preservation, and guaranteed delivery. What a rich blessing the Holy Spirit is! We need to open our hearts to the Him, not just right now, but each and every day.

Day Seventeen
Our Promise Ring

> *...The Holy Spirit of promise, who is the guarantee of our inheritance until the redemption of the purchased possession, to the praise of His glory.*
>
> *Ephesians 1:13-14*

When you receive salvation and you know Christ, even nature becomes more of a blessing. I get a kick out of some of the animals that the Lord has made. My wife Cathy has set up feeders in our yard that attract birds all the time, and these birds are so interesting. There's a woodpecker that pecks, and we always say, "What a strong beak that guy must have!" If you've ever gone snorkeling in Hawaii, you have seen all the wonderfully colorful fish. Even a trip to the local zoo shows you the amazing creativity of our Lord. It's great to enjoy what He has made.

In one of my favorite poems, Wade Robinson writes:

Heaven above is softer blue,
  Earth around is sweeter green,
Something lives in every hue
  That Christless eyes have never seen.
Birds with gladder songs overflow,
  Flowers with deeper beauty shine,
Since I know as now I know,
  I am His and He is mine.[2]

Part of our inheritance in Christ is being able to fully enjoy His creation. This is living abundantly.

You possess true life as a Christian because Christ is life. He came that we might have life abundantly (John 10: 10). He said, I am the Life (John 14:6). And Paul said, "*For to me, to live is Christ...*" (Philippians 1:21). When the Lord is dear to you, it makes life so much sweeter and even the fear of death is taken away. As Paul went on to say in Philippians 1:21, "*...to die is gain.*" He understood that death, though scary, is a small step, and then you're looking at Jesus. Think of it. When you breathe your last breath, with the next one you will be looking into the eyes of Jesus. I have been with a few people who have died. Their breathing gets slower and slower, and then there is the last one. With Christians, you know that they are looking at Jesus right then. That is our hope, and it is a sure hope. We are going right through that veil, as Stephen did when he was stoned. He said, "*Look! I see the heavens opened and the Son of Man standing at the right hand of God*" (Acts 7:56). Wow! Even death belongs to us. Paul says in 1 Corinthians 3:22, "*...things present or things to come—all are yours.*" In other words, everything is in Christ's hands, and He causes all things to work for good to those who love Him and are called according to His purpose (Romans 8:28). This is part of our inheritance. In fact, every promise in the Bible is part of the inheritance that He wants you to lay claim to and grab hold of.

The future belongs to Jesus. He said, "*Now when these things begin to happen, look up and lift up your heads, because your redemption draws near*" (Luke 21:28). "*...Know that it is near—right at the doors!*" (Mark 13:29). Jesus is ready to come, get His bride, and give us the rest of our inheritance.

How do we know He is going to come through? Well, Ephesians 1:14 says that God has put a guarantee on that inheritance, the Holy Spirit. The word guarantee is interesting. In the King James translation, it says an "earnest" of our inheritance, and in Greek, the word is *arrhabon.* It means "earnest money as used in a down payment, guaranteeing that the full payment will be made."

If you have ever purchased a house, you know that you must put down earnest money. You might go into a house that is for sale and say to the person who is selling the house, "You know, I am really interested in this house. Will you hold it for me?" But they are not going to unless you put money down. God is so earnest about giving us our full inheritance that He has given us as a down payment the Holy Spirit. If the Holy Spirit is just a down payment of what our inheritance is, can you imagine what the full inheritance is going to be like?

The Holy Spirit is our comforter. He is our teacher. He empowers us. He gives us joy. He pours out the love of God in our hearts every day. This is our inheritance. The Holy Spirit is a down payment. That's amazing! I can hardly wait for the rest.

Now, in this verse the Greek word *arrhabon* is translated "guarantee." To this day in Greece, *arrabona* means "engagement ring." When a man wants to get engaged to a woman, he gives her a guarantee, which is an engagement ring. Usually a guy is getting pretty serious if he gives you an engagement ring. By this time, the gal has probably been wondering when he's going to ask her to marry him, or more importantly, when he's going to give her a ring. Guys tend to be cheap. You know a guy is getting serious if he puts some money into that ring.

I have a problem with not being romantic enough or doing things in a classy way. Many guys have this problem. The romantic fellas are really blessed and so are their wives, but unfortunately, I'm not. When Cathy and I were going out and I was going to ask her to marry me, I took her to a Chinese greasy spoon in a poor neighborhood. I hate to admit I was that cheap, but every time we go by, Cathy says to the kids, "That's where your Dad asked me to marry him." It seemed romantic enough to me at the time, and since she said yes....

Anyway, I didn't give her a ring at the time; so later, I gave her a beautiful solid gold ring designed like a grapevine with a diamond in the middle of it. The diamond was so small, it took a microscope to see it (I actually got a bigger diamond later), but it was all I could afford at the time. It meant I was committed, I was going to marry her, and everything I had was hers.

Christ has given us His very Spirit, His presence filling our lives. What a guarantee. What an act of love. And this is such a wonderful thing because the Holy Spirit is continually pouring out the love of God in our hearts.

You may say, "I don't often feel the love of Jesus." Well then, tune into the Holy Spirit. Ask the Lord to help you really know and sense the love of God that is pouring into your life. He wants you to be assured. It says in 1 Corinthians 2:9, "*Eye has not seen, nor ear heard, nor have entered into the heart of man the things which God has prepared for those who love Him.*" That is our inheritance, so many "things." You might say, "Yeah, but that is in heaven." It is not just in heaven, it is also now that He wants to show us these things. Verse 10 goes on to say, "*But God has revealed them to us through His Spirit. For the Spirit searches all things, yes, the deep things of God.*" In other words, He has given us the Holy Spirit to show us the thousands of promises in His Word for us to grasp and claim. Not for selfish benefit, but for entering into what He has for us so that we can be a light revealing His goodness to others. The Holy Spirit shows us day by day the wonders and the blessings of God. This is our inheritance.

Day Eighteen
Accessing Our Wealth

Therefore I also, after I heard of your faith in the Lord Jesus and your love for all the saints, do not cease to give thanks for you, making mention of you in my prayers.

Ephesians 1:15-16

The late William Randolph Hearst was a very wealthy newspaper tycoon. One of his hobbies was to invest in and collect prized pieces of art from around the world. On one occasion, a description of some very valuable pieces of art came to his attention, and he decided that he had to have them. He sent his agent overseas to try to track down these pieces of art, and this agent searched and searched. For months, the man sought out the location of these precious treasures of art. Finally, after a year, he located them and immediately called back his employer. "Mr. Hearst, I've found where these treasures are located. They are in your storehouse in San Francisco. You already own them. They belong to you." Hearst hadn't even realized it. All the while, they were his. For months, if he would have just known that they were in his warehouse gathering dust, he could have brought them out and enjoyed them. But they didn't do him any good because he hadn't even checked the listing of his own treasures.

We have been studying the treasures and riches of blessings that are ours spiritually in Jesus Christ. We have spent days looking at them and yet, though these are ours as believers and we know about them, many times we don't lay hold of them by faith, we don't experience them. We leave our Bibles on the shelf gathering dust, and sometimes our faith is dusty as well.

Paul was not content to just let his readers have a listing of those spiritual riches. He wanted them to experience and enjoy them. He, therefore, goes on to pray for them that they will: 1) take hold of what belongs to them; 2) experience the hope of His calling; 3) know the rich and full knowledge of Jesus Christ; 4) enter into the power that belongs to them in Jesus Christ to give them victory in their lives; and 5) know of the riches of His inheritance. All of those things he prays for because he wants to pray into them what he has just told them about.

Many of us are parents. Some of us are teachers. Others are preachers, witnesses, or disciplers of younger Christians. It is not enough just to teach and preach to people about what God has for them. For them to really experience it, we need to pray that they will grab onto it. People aren't necessarily going to lay hold of everything that you tell them. That's true with your kids, right? There is that saying, "You can lead a horse to water, but you can't make him drink." It works that way with people too. However, the neat thing is we can pray that they will drink, that God will give them a thirst, and through prayer, we can actually splash living water on them (so to speak). The Lord will truly reveal Himself, and the Spirit will open their hearts.

Pray for your children. It has been impressed on me so much to pray for my children, diligently, unceasingly. Sometimes we wonder why they don't follow in what we've taught them or how they have been raised. Well, pray. Pray. If you're a teacher, pray for your students. When you witness, pray for those to whom you are witnessing.

Paul is known as a great preacher, a great speaker, and a great writer. Why was he so great as a minister? Because he was a great pray-er. That is why he was so effective and so powerful because God was working through his speaking and through his sharing. God was doing the work. That is what prayer accomplishes.

In Ephesians 1:15-16, Paul starts us off with the first of his awesome prayers, "*Therefore I also, after I heard of your faith in the Lord Jesus and your love for all the saints, do not cease to give thanks for you, making mention of you in my prayers.*" Paul heard of the Ephesians' faith in the Lord Jesus and of their love for Christians. We see here that faith in Christ and love for Christians are linked together. Faith and love—believing in Jesus Christ and loving His people are inseparable. The reason is clear: when you believe in Jesus Christ, it allows you to have God in your life.

First John 4:16 says, "*God is love.*" God is a God of eternal, ultimate love. That is Jesus Christ. And when He comes into our lives, naturally it is going to affect us in loving other people. Faith in God leads to love for people because that is who God is. God loves people. God may hate sin, but He still loves those who commit that sin. We are to love. The love that He gives us is going to enable us to love people.

If your religion has led you to hate people, there is something wrong. Your god can't be the God of the Bible. Your god can't be the God of our Lord Jesus Christ. Your god can't be He who taught us about God and His character. The impact of God upon my life has been love for other people. And Jesus made it especially clear that one of the marks of His true disciples is love for one another (John 13:35).

Paul speaks of the Ephesians' love for all the saints. Who are the saints? They are those who also truly believe in Jesus Christ and know Him. It's not just certain holy people who become saints. No. The biblical definition of saints refers to those who believe in Christ. It says that Paul had heard of the Ephesians' faith in the Lord Jesus and their love for all the saints. Notice that he says, "*all the saints.*" Not just the lovable saints, the lovely saints, or the saints who had loved them back. No. It was "*all the saints.*" Not just the saints in their church, but all the saints, even those who went to other churches.

It's really important that the love we have from Jesus Christ goes out to all of our brothers and sisters whom God brings into our lives or across our paths. We need to love all of them, even if they don't go to our church. That's okay, if they know Christ and love Him, there is a bond. We are brothers and sisters; we are going to spend eternity together.

This is so important because when we get to heaven, God is not going to say, "Okay, all the Baptists over here, all the Presbyterians down there, and (of course) all you Calvary-ites right down here in front." That's not the way it will be because we are all simply believers and lovers of Christ. We are one body, as the Bible says in 1 Corinthians 12:12. We are not better than other Christians, and we are not lesser than other Christians. We are one.

Day Nineteen
Fine Clothes of Thankfulness

...Do not cease to give thanks for you, making mention of you in my prayers.

Ephesians 1:16

Paul begins his prayer with thanksgiving. He doesn't begin with a big shopping list of requests, but he starts out praising and thanking God for His blessings. The biggest blessings we have in life are those who are dear to us—people, relationships, and the family of God. Can you imagine what this world would be like without being together with the family of God, without people who have a kindred heart with whom you can worship God? Nowhere else than with God's people and in His church can you go and just praise the Lord. It's there that people aren't going to look at you and think you're weird.

If you went to work tomorrow at Microsoft and started singing, "I love you Lord, and I lift my voice," your coworkers would call a psychologist, as if you needed your head examined! But that won't happen at church because God's love is there, and He is real. We come together and fellowship. How dark and cold the world would be without God's family. Often, when you don't see people for a while, you realize how much you appreciate them. You become more thankful for them. If you don't see them anymore, you're sad. Paul is away from the Ephesian Christians, writing them from a lonely prison in Rome. He hasn't seen them in a long time, and he is sad. But every time he thinks of them, his heart is filled with thanksgiving. So he thinks of them all the time and tells them, "*I do not cease to give thanks for you, making mention of you in my prayers.*"

We have a tendency, when we think of people, to think negative, critical thoughts. It's easy to do; it can be a natural tendency. Why do you think God brings people to your mind during the day? I have a feeling it's not so you can be critical, although that may be how the thought presents itself. God may be telling you to pray for that person, or if it is a good thought, to thank Him for them. Even if your thoughts are critical, thank God for that person. Certainly, God has some positive reason for bringing them to mind, and I think the reason is prayer. He wants us to intercede on their behalf.

Okay, here's my request: Whenever I come to your mind, and I will, pray for me. Whenever you come to my mind, and you do, I will pray for you. I want you to do that for each other. Whenever you think of someone, pray that God will bless them. And if you believe you see a major fault in their life, pray for that too. They need that.

I have found that if I decide to give thanks and clothe myself with a thankful heart in expressing gratitude to God about people, it helps me repent of being critical. I have that problem sometimes. Maybe you have that problem sometimes too. When you think of those people, the best remedy is to thank God and pray for them. This is how we learn to be thankful and graceful people.

Thankfulness is a learned attitude. Have you noticed that with your children? You have to teach them to be thankful. They don't just automatically thank those who do nice things for them.

"Now, Johnny, thank Mrs. Smith for her gift to you."

"Thank you, Mrs. Smith."

We hope that eventually it sinks in (sometimes it does). But it is a learned thing. Our heavenly Father wants to teach us thankfulness. Paul is thanking God for them, and this is his first priority in prayer.

Day Twenty

The Value of Knowing Our Father - Part 1

> *...That the God of our Lord Jesus Christ, the Father of glory, may give to you the spirit of wisdom and revelation in the knowledge of Him...*
>
> *Ephesians 1:17*

The first and most important aspect of prayer is knowing to whom you are talking. We are talking to God. Paul addresses God here as "*the Father of glory...*" Above everything else that Jesus taught us about God, He taught us that He is our heavenly Father. I love that. Knowing that God is omnipotent, pure, holy, and perfect can be a little scary, until I remember that He is my heavenly Father. More than 180 times in the gospels, God is referred to as our Father in heaven. Over 100 times in the Gospel of John, Jesus taught us that God is our Father in heaven. He even taught us to call Him "Abba, Father," which means "papa" or "daddy." I can come to Him. He loves me. He is my heavenly Father. He is an all-loving Father. Maybe you didn't have a loving earthly father, but your heavenly Father is. That is such an encouragement.

When Paul calls God "*the Father of glory,*" it makes me think of the glorious presence that traveled and dwelt with the children of Israel when they walked through the wilderness. His glory dwelt with them when they came into the Promised Land. That glorious presence was God Himself, and He lived in the Holy of Holies. That glory, the *shekinah*, is an intense presence of the Lord.

Do you ever feel that *shekinah* glory in your relationship with God? Sometimes there is a kind of heavenly presence. You don't always feel it; you don't even feel it often. But sometimes you do. The truth is, His presence is always there. You can always be certain of His presence whether you feel it or not. He said, "*I will never leave you nor forsake you*" (Hebrews 13:5). Jesus said, "*...I am with you always, even to the end of the age*" (Matthew 28:20).

He is the Father of glory. His glorious presence dwells with us. In Ephesians 1:17, Paul makes the request that the Father of glory "*may give to you the spirit of wisdom and revelation in the knowledge of Him.*" This is his first and most important prayer request and the basis for every other. The request is that you might know Him, or more to the point, that you might be filled with the knowledge of Him.

This word knowledge in Greek is the word *epignosis*. *Gnosis* means "knowledge," but *epignosis* means "a full and true knowledge." It is so important for us to have a true knowledge of God. Sometimes you think you know someone, but later you find out you didn't truly know them. It's a sad revelation at times, but other times you're glad. It is important for us to have a true knowledge of God because a false or inaccurate view can hurt your faith and seriously damage your understanding of God. Just ask someone who has been involved in a cult. It can really mess you up if you don't have a true knowledge of God. Cults take certain Scriptures to an extreme and use them to oppress their followers with a twisted knowledge of God. But you won't be deceived if you have a true knowledge of God.

That's why it is so important to have an overall, solid understanding of the Bible, not just a grasp of certain little things. We really need to dig in and learn the balance of Scripture. We need to know the whole Bible. Within Scripture is the knowledge of God, and it gives us that balance. Jesus said to the Pharisees, "*You search the Scriptures, for in them you think you have eternal life; and these are they which testify of Me*" (John 5:39). In other words, they were using religion to be self-righteous, prideful, and exclusive, and they were missing the real point. Jesus was saying it's all about Him, and they didn't even know Him. So we should study the Bible in order to truly get to know God, for that is the primary purpose of Scripture. God wants to show us Himself; He wants us to know Him as we learn the Bible.

I know my wife, Cathy, very well. One day, a lady came up to me and complained about Cathy. She told me all this stuff that my wife had supposedly said. But I know my wife, and I know Cathy wouldn't say those things, so I rebuked this lady. I said, "You are wrong. She never said that. She never did that." Later, I talked to Cathy about it, and she said, "No, it never happened." The lady had been lying or misunderstanding something. How did I know that? Simple—I know my wife.

Some voice may come to you and say God is mad at you or disgusted with you. That is not true. God's love does not waver or fluctuate. God is immutable; He doesn't change. And God is holy and righteous and faithful. When we learn what God is like from His Word, it will help us have a true relationship with Him.

Day Twenty-One
The Value of Knowing Our Father - Part 2

> *...That the God of our Lord Jesus Christ, the Father of glory, may give to you the spirit of wisdom and revelation in the knowledge of Him...*
>
> Ephesians 1:17

Full knowledge is very important for having full enjoyment. The more you know God, the more you love God. And we can always learn more about God. Paul said, "*Yet indeed I also count all things loss for the excellence of the knowledge of Christ Jesus my Lord, for whom I have suffered the loss of all things, and count them as rubbish, that I may gain Christ and be found in Him...*" (Philippians 3:8-9). Knowing Jesus is the greatest treasure in the whole world. Everything else is a bunch of garbage in comparison.

You have to put time into knowing someone. Of course, it's worth it when they're wonderful people. I hope you are taking time to know God more than anyone else. Paul prayed for the Ephesians to have knowledge of God. In fact, he prayed that God would give them "*the spirit of wisdom and revelation in the knowledge of Him.*" We could not even know God unless He revealed Himself to us.

In Luke 10:22, Jesus said, "*...no one knows who the Son is except the Father, and who the Father is except the Son, and the one to whom the Son wills to reveal Him.*" So God will give us a spirit of revelation to know Him. Christ reveals Him (John 1:18). Think of it. Almighty God wants to reveal Himself to you. That's why when you believe in Christ, He gives you the Holy Spirit. In 1 Corinthians 2:11, Paul says, "*For what man knows the things of a man except the spirit of the man which is in him? Even so no one knows the things of God except the Spirit of God.*" The Spirit of God knows everything about God, and He has been given to us to show us God and to reveal those things freely given to us by God.

That is one of the blessings of having the Holy Spirit. He is God, He is with you, and He wants to show you something new about Himself every day. I love to learn new things about the people I like. And it has been the greatest joy of all to get to know God.

What effect should this have on our lives then? It should encourage us to be pure. For example, 1 John 3:2-3 says, "*Beloved, now we are children of God; and it has not yet been revealed what we shall be, but we know that when He is revealed, we shall be like Him, for we shall see Him as He is. And everyone who has this hope in Him purifies himself, just as He is pure.*"

One of the topics that I love to study is Bible prophecy. It really reveals God's love to me because Christ is coming back for us. But it also makes me want to be holy; it makes me want to be pure because I have this hope. Since He could come at any time, I want to purify my life so I won't be ashamed at His coming.

I know many people who are fascinated by Bible prophecy. If you ask them what's the latest on Bible prophecy, they know everything. They read all the Bible prophecy gurus. They are up on all the latest happenings in the Middle East. But have they missed the main theme of the Bible? We need to be working on knowing Jesus and walking with Christ, not just knowing Bible prophecy. They may go around saying "He is probably going to come on such and such a date." Don't get into that stuff. He will come when He chooses to come. It will be soon, and He wants you to know that. Live like it will be soon, but don't get into the whole date thing. Just be ready and purify yourself with that hope.

Other people want to know how to have a successful marriage. The Bible talks about that. It is one of the Bible's themes.

But what about knowing Jesus?

Some only want to know how to be free from fear, stress, and depression. There is a lot about that in the Bible too.

But what about knowing God?

Knowing God is the Bible's main theme. In fact, when people come to me and say they have this problem, they have that problem, their marriage is thus and so, I tell them, "You need to get to know Jesus because as Christ loves you, you are to love your wife. Have you been receiving the love of Jesus lately? Has your relationship in Him been growing? You don't need a book on marriage. You need to repent, draw near to Jesus, and get close to Him."

I am not saying books on marriage are bad. I am saying the best book on marriage is the Bible, the Word of God. The best thing for our marriage is to be filled with the love of Jesus. Knowing God is the best way to be free from worry. Have God lift your burden. Do you see why the knowledge of His Word is so important? It is everything, and everything comes from it.

When Crowfoot, the great chief of the Blackfoot Indian Confederacy in southern Alberta, gave the Canadian Pacific Railroad permission to cross the Blackfoot land from Medicine Hat to Calgary, he was given in return a lifetime railroad pass. Crowfoot put it in a leather case and carried it around his neck for the rest of his life. However, the sad fact is there is no record that he ever traveled anywhere on a Canadian Pacific train.

The promises of God are often treated in this way by Christians. We hang them on our walls written on beautiful plaques, but we do not claim His promises for ourselves in times of need. Of what use is God's Word on plaques if it's not applied to our lives?

Day Twenty-Two
Diamond Clarity

> *...The eyes of your understanding being enlightened; that you may know what is the hope of His calling, what are the riches of the glory of His inheritance in the saints...*
>
> *Ephesians 1:18*

Awhile back, our cat, Soot, had a litter of kittens. When kittens are born, they're blind. Their eyelids don't open for a week or two, so they have to feel around in order to nurse, snuggle, and stay warm. It's always a great day when their eyes finally open. All of sudden they can see their mom, their brothers and sisters, and their pestering masters (our sons, Nick and Riley). They can see the wonders of their new world. That's important because cats rely on keen eyesight. Cats have something called a tapetum behind their retina that reflects all the incoming light, so it goes through twice. This helps them to see in very dim light and even in darkness, which is vital for their survival.

Paul knew that spiritual eyesight is essential. Only as the eyes of our hearts are enlightened are we able to understand the treasure we have in Christ. Knowing the Lord Jesus Christ is the greatest gift of all, and Paul realized this knowledge would open up all the other blessings of the Christian life.

In Jeremiah 9:23-24, the Lord declared, "*Let not the wise man glory in his wisdom, let not the mighty man glory in his might, nor let the rich man glory in his riches; but let him who glories glory in this, that he understands and knows Me, that I am the LORD.*" Now that's what you should really revel in! You have a relationship with Jesus Christ, and you know His ways.

Knowing God brings true enlightenment because God is light. First John 1:5-6 says, "*...God is light and in Him is* *no darkness at all. If we say that we have fellowship with Him, and walk in darkness, we lie and do not practice the truth.*" Only God can light up your life and light up your understanding of life. It's like coming into the sunshine when you've been in darkness and gloom. You let the Word of God and the presence of Jesus dispel the darkness. When you know God, the eyes of your heart become enlightened. The light of God shines on the deepest part of your being and brightens it up.

In Scripture, light represents holiness rather than evil; love rather than hate; truth rather than deception. Nothing needs to be brightened up more than the human heart and mind. It can be a very dark place. The Bible says the heart is deceitful and desperately wicked (Jeremiah 17:9).

Even as Christians, we can allow the darkness of our flesh and the carnal mind to take over. In Ephesians 4:17-18, we are told it is alienation from God that brings about darkened understanding. Ignorance of God keeps people in the dark. When we block out the knowledge of Christ and go after temptation, even though God is faithful to provide a way of escape, we darken our minds and hearts. Don't go that way!

Every day, you have the privilege of letting the sunshine in. On a bright sunny day, you're not going to pull the shades, shut the curtains, and live in darkness. In the same way, spiritually we need to open the shades and let the light in. Let the hope, joy, and love of the Lord in.

How do you do this? You do it by reading His Word. It opens the shades. You do it through prayer, and the light of His presence comes into your life. In John 8:12, Jesus said, "*I am the light of the world. He who follows Me shall not walk in darkness, but have the light of life.*" This is the true enlightenment, knowing Christ. Most of the people you hear talking about enlightenment today are caught up in deception. But when you know the Christ of the Bible, your mind and heart are enlightened. You can see a whole new realm, a whole new part of the world that you didn't even know about, namely God. You see that spiritual things are real, angels and demons are real, and our adversary the devil is real. He really deceives. You find out the difference between sin and what's right, between impurity and holiness. These spiritual truths all of a sudden become real to you.

Many years ago, a poor man in North Carolina was walking along a well-traveled path next to a stream called Limpid Brook. Like many others before him, he noticed a big, unsightly boulder in the middle of the brook, but while others passed by with indifference, this man thought, "Hey, I could use that boulder to hold my front door open. It would make a great doorstop!" So he took the boulder home. One day, a geologist walked by his house, noticed the boulder, and stopped to check it out. It turned out to be a huge lump of gold—the biggest lump of gold ever found east of the Rockies. All of a sudden, that poor man became very wealthy.

Those of us who are in Jesus live in a spiritual goldmine of wisdom and wealth. Knowing Christ and His Word opens up a whole new world of light, truth, hope, love, and God's power and grace.

Day Twenty-Three
The Gem of Our Hope

> *...The eyes of your understanding being enlightened; that you may know what is the hope of His calling, what are the riches of the glory of His inheritance in the saints...*
>
> *Ephesians 1:18*

Hope is the light we all need. As a Christian, you can always have hope. Of course, having said that, we tend to feel guilty when we don't feel hopeful. But truly, you do have hope!

What is our hope? Titus 2:13 says, we are "*looking for the blessed hope and glorious appearing of our great God and Savior Jesus Christ...*" Our hope is sure, but what we see in this world is not it. This world is not all there is; if it is, there is not much hope. But God's kingdom is real, and His coming is sure. He promised us over and over again He would come. That is our hope.

God promised us that Messiah would come the first time, and He did, and He has promised us that He is going to come again. This is our great and sure hope, and we eagerly look forward to it. There are many aspects of this hope, but it basically boils down to two things. First, one of these days, we are going to see Jesus face to face. We are going to be looking right into His eyes. Right now, we are apart from Him physically, although spiritually, He is right here. Jesus says, "*For where two or three are gathered together in My name, I am there in the midst of them*" (Matthew 18:20). He is in our hearts if we know Him, even though we are apart from Him physically.

Revelation 22:4 says one day we shall look upon His face. I hope and believe it will be one day soon. On that day, our Lord is not going to be speaking as we've heard Him here with that quiet inner voice. We are going to actually hear the audible trumpet-voice of Jesus, shouting because He is so excited to come. In Mark 13:29, Jesus tells us that when we see certain signs taking place, we know that He is right at the door. He is anxious to come! The trumpet will sound, Christ will descend from heaven, and the dead in Christ will rise first. Then we who are alive and remain will be caught up. Literally, we will be forcefully taken up in a moment, in the twinkling of an eye, and meet the Lord in the air. And so shall we always be with the Lord (1 Thessalonians 4:16-17).

When you are apart from someone you love, you can hardly wait to be reunited, and when you are, you hope that you will never be apart again. That is the way it is going to be. We will never, ever be apart from Jesus again. We will always be with the Lord.

The other main aspect of our hope in Christ's coming is this: when we see Him, we will be just like Him. We will be made in His likeness. It tells us in 1 John 3:2, "*Beloved, now we are children of God; and it has not yet been revealed what we shall be, but we know that when He is revealed, we shall be like Him, for we shall see Him as He is.*" Even now, the more you see Jesus Christ by studying His Word, by walking near to Him, by walking in the Spirit, the more you will be changed. That is how you are changed into His likeness.

But one day you will see Him face to face, and the work will be done. You will be transformed. Our goal and our hope as Christians are not to "be like Mike," as the Michael Jordan commercial says, or any other hero of our time, but to be like Jesus. Think of that! You won't struggle with sin ever again. There will be no reason to worry that you are going to struggle with impatience or anger. Nothing will make you afraid. You will no longer struggle with lust, discouragement, or depression ever again. You will be like Jesus. The Holy Spirit is working to make this hope very real because He is working in your heart to show you how present the Lord is even now. Although apart from Him physically, He wants you to live knowing that He is right with you. He is in you, and the Holy Spirit makes Him more and more real.

As His Spirit works within our hearts, we are transformed from glory to glory into His image (2 Corinthians 3:18). Knowing the hope of His calling really has a great effect on our lives. What does it do? It works in you so that you are never satisfied with the trinkets and trivialities of this world again. You're not going to be laying up your treasures on earth. You're not going to be thinking, "Oh, I can hardly wait to get more of the world's stuff. It is so great, so glamorous." No. Your hope is elsewhere, and it's a different hope. You realize you belong to something so much greater. There is a new world coming. His kingdom is real to you, and your hope is in that world.

Therefore, as John said, don't love the world or the things in the world. Because all that is in the world, the lust of the flesh, the lust of the eyes, the boastful pride of life, these are from the world. They are not from God. They are passing away. But the one who does the will of God lives forever (1 John 2:15-17). So hope makes you want to do the will of God. It makes you want to serve Him, makes you want to build up treasures in Him, makes you want to really invest in lasting things and use the material blessings that God gives you to lay up eternal treasures.

This hope also gives you a fantastic comfort that there is more. This world is not it. Jesus is coming! "*Therefore comfort one another with these words*" (1 Thessalonians 4:18). Yes, the hope of His calling really affects us tremendously. If the things of this world are everything to you, then you are missing out on the true hope of life. If you are caught up in the fleeting pleasures of this world, you need a real glimpse of the hope that is so much greater. Paul prays for that, and we need to pray that for each other. You have a destiny. Invest in it.

Day Twenty-Four
We Are His Pearl

> *...The eyes of your understanding being enlightened; that you may know what is the hope of His calling, what are the riches of the glory of His inheritance in the saints...*
>
> *Ephesians 1:18*

I can hardly believe what this verse says. You'd think Paul would pray that we would know the riches of the glory of our inheritance in Him, but he doesn't say that. He says, "*that you may know...what are the riches of the glory of His inheritance in the saints.*" Yikes! How could that be? I am an inheritance for Jesus? Poor Lord. Yet that is what this verse says.

Ephesians 5:25 says, "*...Christ also loved the church and gave Himself for her, that He might sanctify and cleanse her with the washing of water by the word, that He might present her to Himself a glorious church, not having spot or wrinkle or any such thing, but that she should be holy and without blemish.*" He is working in us to be glorious.

Revelation 19:7-8 says, "*Let us be glad and rejoice and give Him glory, for the marriage of the Lamb has come, and His wife has made herself ready. And to her it was granted to be arrayed in fine linen, clean and bright, for the fine linen is the righteous acts of the saints.*" We are going to be beautiful on that day for Him. He is doing a work. Let's cooperate with Him in that work. We are an inheritance. He values us.

If you find it hard to believe that we are the riches of the glory of His inheritance, read Matthew 13. Jesus told a couple of short parables about some hidden treasure and the pearl of great price: "*Again, the kingdom of heaven is like treasure hidden in a field, which a man found and hid; and for joy over it he goes and sells all that he has and buys that field. Again, the kingdom of heaven is like a merchant seeking beautiful pearls, who, when he had found one pearl of great price, went and sold all that he had and bought it*" (Matthew 13:44-46). These parables are amazing. The hidden treasure and the pearl of great price are not referring to Jesus (although He is a glorious treasure, a pearl of exquisite value, and we should give up everything to follow and serve Him). The reason we know these parables are not referring to Him is because we can't sell everything and buy Jesus. He can't be bought because He is free. Rather, He is the merchant in these parables. The Lord sold everything to buy us. The field in the parable is the world, and the hidden treasure in the field is the church. He bought the whole field. He so loved the world that He gave His only begotten Son (John 3:16). The believers are His treasure. You are His hidden treasure. You are His pearl of great price.

I love J. Vernon McGee's commentary on this pearl of great price:

> Now let's look at the pearl for a moment. The pearl represents the church. A pearl is not a stone like the diamond. It is formed by a living organism, an oyster. A grain of sand or other foreign matter intrudes itself into the shell of a small sea creature. It hurts and harms the creature. The response of the organism is to send out a secretion that coats over the foreign matter, coats over the grain of sand. That fluid builds up until a pearl is formed. Not a ruby or a diamond, but a beautiful, white pearl. Listen to this application. Christ came to this earth as the merchantman. He saw a man in sin and He took man's sin and He bore it in His own body. Our sin was an intrusion upon Jesus. It was that foreign matter. He was made sin for us. As someone has put it, I got into the heart of Christ by a spear wound. Christ was wounded for our transgressions. Notice Christ's response to the sinner. He puts around us His own righteousness. He covers us with His own white robe of righteousness. We are His workmanship created

> in Christ Jesus. Christ sees us, not as we are now, but as we shall be someday—a glorious church, not having spot or wrinkle or any such thing, but that we should be holy and without blemish, like a pearl. Christ sold all that He had in order that He might gain the church, this beautiful gem. Praise God! This is how He views you as a believer and this is the work that He is doing.[3]

I hope the fact that He values us and that He is working in us in such a glorious way makes us want to be all that we can be for Him, to let His Holy Spirit purify our lives, and to let Him use us to show His glory. I hope it makes us want to set ourselves apart for His coming. Let's set ourselves apart spiritually and morally in all that we do as singles or as marrieds until He comes. I love it when Christian singles or Christian young people keep themselves pure and set themselves apart for the future spouse who is going to be theirs. We need to have that attitude for Jesus, for He is our Glorious Groom who is coming soon. I hope His love motivates you to be all that you can be for Him.

Day Twenty-Five
His Treasured Power

> *...That you may know...what is the exceeding greatness of His power toward us who believe, according to the working of His mighty power...*
>
> *Ephesians 1:18-19*

Today, let's look at the exceeding great power of God that is toward us who believe. There is this tremendous and practical strength and power that God wants us as believers to experience.

Years ago, I went outside on my porch in Seattle on a beautiful, sunny spring morning. It was about 8:30, and I was breathing in the fresh air, when all of a sudden I heard a huge explosion. I thought, "What on earth was that?" Then I looked to the south and saw this gigantic billowing mushroom cloud going up into the sky. My first thought was, "Oh no, we've been attacked! It's a nuclear explosion!" But I was wrong. The date was May 18, 1980, and Mount St. Helens was blowing her top.

Mount St. Helens blew with the power of 500 Hiroshima atom bombs, or 10 million tons of dynamite. The top 1,300 feet of that volcano was blown right off. A single blast, heated to 300 degrees Fahrenheit, moving at 200 miles per hour down the mountain, mowed down everything in its path and leveled a forest of trees for 17 miles. Not just little trees, but big 150-foot Douglas firs. That is 3.2 billion board feet of lumber, enough to build 200,000, three-bedroom homes. What an awesome release of power!

Jesus said in Mark 11:22-23, "*So Jesus answered and said to them, 'Have faith in God. For assuredly, I say to you, whoever says to this mountain, "Be removed and be cast into the sea," and does not doubt in his heart, but believes that those things he says will come to pass, he will have whatever he says."'* The Lord wasn't talking about blowing up physical mountains. He was talking about the mountains of difficulty, problems, or challenges that we face. He wants to give us power, not to destroy or ruin, but to redeem and transform. And Paul prays that we may know what that power is and that we may experience it.

Paul is really praying a mouthful in Ephesians 1:19, "[That you may know]...*what is the exceeding greatness of His power toward us who believe, according to the working of His mighty power.*" When you read this verse in the original Greek language, it is so graphic. The word exceeding, *huperballo*, means "limitless." Greatness, *megethos*, means "big," from which we get the word megaton. The word power is *dunamis*, meaning "dynamic," or "dynamite power." According to the working is *energeia*, or "energizing." The second word for power in verse 19 is *kratos*, which means "vigor," and the word for mighty power means "forceful." So we could translate this verse, "That you may know what is the limitless megaton-age of His dynamite power toward us who believe according to the energizing of His forceful vigor." Wow! That's the power of God, the power of Jesus Christ.

With such power available to us to help and strengthen, you'd think that our first thought would always be to depend on God, to ask God for help, to cry out to Him. But, in fact, it's not. Many times, we don't call upon Him; we don't look to Him. And why don't we? Well, I am sure there are many reasons, but it boils down to self-sufficiency. Either we think He doesn't want to help us, or we think, "I'll do it myself. I can do it. I don't need help." That's why one of the best teachers in our lives is failure, not being able to do it. When we fail, we see ourselves as we really are, weak and in dire need of God's help. That's a good thing.

Failure is not the worst thing that could happen to you. What would be even worse is thinking that you could go through life without depending on God, without needing God. You can go through life that way, but you won't excel the way God wants you to. You can't flourish in doing God's will without His help. You are not as good a husband as God wants you to be unless you trust in Him and depend upon Him. You're not as good of a wife, or a parent, or whatever you are, without Christ. Though you may be great, you're not as great as God could make you in true greatness. You need the Lord's help.

Therefore, through failure we learn that we are imperfect, we are weak; but we learn that He is strong. That's why Paul said he was glad when these things came along to show him his weakness. When I realize my weakness, I see that His power is perfected in that weakness (2 Corinthians 12:9-10).

Zerubbabel learned that lesson. He was the governor of Israel who was rebuilding the temple that had been destroyed. The temple was in a mountain of rubble, and he was trying to get it rebuilt. Every time he made an effort, enemies would come in and thwart the work, making it an impossible task. It was just a mess. And then the Lord used Zechariah as the Holy Spirit spoke through him saying, "*This is the word of the LORD to Zerubbabel: 'Not by might nor by power, but by My Spirit,' says the LORD of hosts. 'Who are you, O great mountain? Before Zerubbabel you shall become a plain! And he shall bring forth the capstone [of the temple] with shouts of "Grace, grace to it!"'*" (Zechariah 4:6-7).

It's not by might, that is it's not by human strength. It's not by power. It's not by human ability. But it's by My Spirit says the Lord. That's not a put down. I don't think Zerubbabel is thinking, "Oh, sure, thanks! You think I can't do it." No, it's an encouragement. It's a comfort. You don't have to do it on your own. You don't have to be the one to pull yourself up by your own bootstraps all the time. You were created to depend on God. You were created to look to God. God wants to help. He wants to do it. He wants to show you Himself. As Zerubbabel looked at that huge mountain and that impossible task, he took heart. He thought, "God is with me; God is for me; God wants to work." And God did work. They rebuilt the temple, and when Zerubbabel put the capstone on, he proclaimed, "It's God's grace."

Day Twenty-Six
A Wealth of Power - Part 1

> *...And what is the exceeding greatness of His power toward us who believe, according to the working of His mighty power which He worked in Christ when He raised Him from the dead and seated Him at His right hand in the heavenly places...*
>
> *Ephesians 1:19-20*

There are some great verses in Ephesians that talk about the power of God shown at the resurrection and what that power means for us. First, in Ephesians 1:19-20, Paul prays that you may know "*what is the exceeding greatness of His power toward us who believe, according to the working of His mighty power which He worked in Christ when He raised Him from the dead and seated Him at His right hand in the heavenly places...*" Then in Ephesians 2:5-6, "*...even when we were dead in trespasses, made us alive together with Christ (by grace you have been saved), and raised us up together, and made us sit together in the heavenly places in Christ Jesus.*"

Someone might ask, "If Jesus rose from the dead and He is still alive, where is He? I haven't seen Him lately. He wasn't on NBC Nightly News in the last year. Larry King hasn't interviewed Him. Where is He? If He is risen, if He is still alive, if this is an actual literal truth, then where is He?"

That's a good question to ask! Let's consider. Jesus Christ was crucified, died for our sins, and was buried. Then He powerfully rose from the dead and began appearing to people. Again and again, over a period of 40 days, He showed Himself alive. He appeared to many different groups of people, a total of well over 500 different individuals. This happened on at least 15 separate occasions over a period of 40 days with many convincing proofs. These appearances were written down by eyewitnesses and documented for all future generations.

Then something happened that's almost as powerful as the resurrection itself. Jesus, in His last appearance, walked with His disciples over to the little town of Bethany on the Mount of Olives. And while He was talking to His disciples, suddenly He was lifted off the ground, and He was taken up into heaven. He ascended into heaven as they were watching. He went up into a cloud, and He disappeared.

You see, Jesus had told them, "Once I have finished My work and have accomplished salvation for you, I will return to My heavenly Father, sit again at His right hand, and send My Holy Spirit to dwell within you" (John 14 paraphrased). Imagine what the disciples must have felt as they watched Jesus take off into heaven. Man, their eyes must have been like saucers! In fact, a couple of angels standing by said, "*Men of Galilee, why do you stand gazing up into heaven? This same Jesus, who was taken up from you into heaven, will so come in like manner as you saw Him go into heaven*" (Acts 1:11).

I still love to watch the space shuttle take off. It is so incredible; there is so much power. In fact, most of the space shuttle's power comes from those big external tanks of fluid and the solid rocket boosters. At launch, those external tanks are burning 816 gallons of fuel per second. And 1.5 million pounds of fuel is burned up just to launch it. There are 3.4 million pounds of thrusting power from the solid rocket boosters just to get that thing into orbit. But the space shuttle is only 122 feet long. It's so small, after it lands, it's returned to Florida on the back of a Boeing 747.

Jesus didn't need solid rocket boosters to raise from the dead. He didn't need liquid hydrogen and oxygen fuel to launch Him into heaven because He wasn't demonstrating the power of man's accomplishments. He was demonstrating that greatest of all powers, the power of God Himself. Jesus was showing that God is real. He was an example to us of the reality of God, and He wants to bring us into a relationship with God. His power is so great and so pure. Paul prayed that you would know "*what is the exceeding greatness of*

His power toward us who believe." When we believe in Jesus Christ, God lifts our lives out of the pit of sin and selfishness and gives us spiritual wings to rise and live above it. "*For the law of the Spirit of life in Christ Jesus has made me free from the law of sin and death*" (Romans 8:2).

I read a story about Alexander the Great in which this poor and needy man came up to Alexander's throne and asked him for relief from his deprivation. So Alexander wrote the man a treasury note to receive any amount he should ask for. Well, the man went to the treasurer and ordered 100,000 gold pieces. The treasurer told him, "No way, that's far too extravagant a request." However, to this, Alexander the Great replied, "Give him all he asks for immediately. The largeness of his request honors me, for it shows that he has a very high opinion of my wealth, my word, and my benevolence."[4]

Even so, the Lord is honored when we have a very high opinion of His riches and His Word. Many people minimize the benefit of receiving God's help and strength for their daily lives. They're only cheating themselves. David said it perfectly in Psalm 3:2-3, "*Many are they who say of me, 'There is no help for him in God.' But You, O LORD, are a shield for me, my glory and the One who lifts up my head.*"

Day Twenty-Seven
A Wealth of Power - Part 2

> *...And what is the exceeding greatness of His power toward us who believe, according to the working of His mighty power which He worked in Christ when He raised Him from the dead and seated Him at His right hand in the heavenly places...*
>
> *Ephesians 1:19-20*

Why do we need the awesome power that God used to raise Christ from the dead? Because we were dead. We were dead in our trespasses and sins. "*But God, who is rich in mercy, because of His great love with which He loved us, even when we were dead in our trespasses, made us alive together with Christ...*" (Ephesians 2:4-5).

The Bible is very clear that this world is a big spiritual graveyard. We have all seen physical graveyards, but the entire earth is a spiritual graveyard full of people who are dead because of sin.

The Bible helps us understand what death is. Death is separation. Physical death is the separation of our spirit and soul from our bodies. We understand that. When a person dies, his body becomes just an empty shell, the soul and the spirit are separated away, and the body is dead. Spiritual death is even worse. It is the separation of our spirit and soul from God. That is spiritual death, and it is caused by sin.

Sin is disobeying God's commands. God created the world, and He created us, so He makes the rules. Many people don't like it, but that's too bad. He is the Creator. When we disobey God, we bring death on ourselves. A lot of people sin while thinking, "This is so great and so fun." The truth is, however, that sin has killed our innocence. It has killed our ideals. It has killed the meaning in life that God wants us to have. And it has killed our sensitivity to God's reality. It has killed us.

Of course, many of us have been to a cemetery, a mortuary, or a funeral parlor where there are dead people. When people are physically dead, they can't respond to physical stimulus. So if you are having a conversation in a funeral parlor, the dead people aren't going to join in. If you are eating food, they aren't going to say, "Hey, give me some," because they no longer have an appetite.

Spiritually, it is like that without Christ. Without Christ, you can't see how real God is. Without Christ, you don't yet see the vast love that God has for you. He wants to show His love to you, but you are spiritually dead. Maybe you don't have much of a hunger for spiritual things. You can't hear God's Word because dead people can't hear. Therefore, the Bible is just some book. And when you bring up God and Jesus to people who aren't born again, it can be a short conversation. It can even be awkward sometimes because they don't have a clue about Him yet. They don't know how real He is. God wants to reveal Himself, but those who don't know Christ are spiritually dead.

As it says in Ephesians 2:5, they are dead in trespasses and sins. All of us were like that without Christ; it's what sin has done to human beings. It has deadened our relationship with God. Violating His commands and our own consciences has brought dullness, shame, and guilt, and we feel that we can't approach God.

This is what happened to Adam and Eve after they ate the forbidden fruit. The Bible says that they went and hid and sewed fig leaves together to cover up their shame (Genesis 3:7). They didn't feel like they could relate to God anymore, even though prior to this they had wonderful fellowship in the garden in the cool of the day. Now, all they had was shame, guilt, and loneliness. Their sin pushed them away from God.

This void, this loneliness remains with us down to the present time. You wonder, "Why do I feel so empty? There is no logical reason for it. Why do I sometimes feel lonely even when people are around?" These thoughts are sure testimony that sin is real, and separation from God because of sin is real.

We are homesick for God. You may not realize it, but you are really homesick inside for the One who loves you most, your Maker. Your life consisted of shame, guilt, loneliness, emptiness, and spiritual death...but then God's love came in. We read in Ephesians 2:4, "*But God, who is rich in mercy, because of His great love with which He loved us...*" I love that phrase, "*But God...*" That makes a big difference. God's love comes on the scene because He has given us a powerful Savior.

In fact, Acts 2:24 says it was impossible for Jesus to be held by death's power. Why? Because He is the Son of God, and He died, not for His own sins, but for my sins and your sins. You see, Jesus has no sin. The only sin Jesus has ever known is my sin and your sin. He took the judgment against our sin upon Himself on the cross, He took the condemnation, and, in a sense, He experienced eternal hell because He is the eternal God. In that moment of time, He took hell's judgment of our sins so that we could be forgiven, cleansed, and given a new life. That new life with God comes from believing in Jesus, believing what He did, repenting of our sin, and receiving Him. What a powerful new life it is. It is life with God!

Day Twenty-Eight
A Wealth of Power - Part 3

> *...And what is the exceeding greatness of His power toward us who believe, according to the working of His mighty power which He worked in Christ when He raised Him from the dead and seated Him at His right hand in the heavenly places...*
>
> Ephesians 1:19-20

I once read a story about a young boy and his dad. As they were driving in the countryside with the windows down and the breezes blowing, this big, huge bee flew into the car. The young boy was highly allergic to bees, to the point where if he was stung, it could kill him. So he became terrified, and rightfully so. He was frantic with fear when his father reached out and grabbed the bee in his hand and squeezed it. Then he let it go.

The bee was still alive and started flying around again. It flew near the boy and again the boy became petrified. But the father reached out his hand to the little boy and said, "Son, look at my hand. See right there? It's the stinger. I took the sting out of the bee. It is in my hand now. It can't hurt you. It's like a big fly now."

That is what Jesus did for us. First Corinthians 15:55-56 says, "'*O death, where is your sting?'...The sting of death is sin...*" Why is sin such a stinger? Because we deserve to be condemned. We deserve to be judged because God is holy. But Jesus on the cross was judged for you and for me. And once that judgment had been paid and Jesus was buried, He rose again, which is the proof that God accepted the sacrifice Jesus made; and He will accept us too if we believe in Him. The sting of spiritual death does not have to hurt you anymore. That is so cool!

How do you know that you can come to a holy God? How do you know God will accept you? How do you know you can have a relationship with God? You know because when God raised Jesus from the dead, it was His declaration that Christ's sacrifice to make us righteous was fully approved. "*Jesus...was delivered up because of our offenses, and was raised because of our justification*" (Romans 4:24-25).

You know, a lot of people really diminish God. They think, "Oh yeah, I know God. He is the nice old guy in the sky, man. He's a cool dude. And if He doesn't accept me, I will tell Him a thing or two." The truth is, if you came into His presence without Christ, you would be fried. He is pure. He is holy. This is the awesome God. But Jesus took the sting and the condemnation out of sin so that we could be raised to eternal life. That broken relationship can now be restored.

How does this happen? It happens when you believe. Believe in Him and personally trust Him that He died for you. And when you receive Him, He'll come in, wash the shame and guilt away, and give you His Spirit. As the Bible says, you are raised to a new life together with Him (Ephesians 2:5-6). That happens when you believe in Him as your own Savior and your own Lord. It says in Ephesians 1:19, "*[That you may know] ...what is the exceeding greatness of His power toward us who believe...*" Jesus has done everything, but we have to believe. It is a small thing, but He requires it. That is the connection that joins you with the living Lord and gives you a new life with God.

I remember one day I came out of my house and went to start my car, like I always do, but this time when I turned the key, nothing happened. I hate that. You turn the key and you're expecting to hear the engine roar, but nothing happens. So I opened the hood, hit the battery, and pulled the cables (because I'm such a great mechanic). Then I tried to start it again...nothing. So I checked the battery, and it was fine; it had power. I checked the ignition switch. I jerked it around a little, wriggled and jiggled it, but still nothing. I got out, looked at the starter, and hit it with a wrench.

Still nothing. Finally, I gave up and just left it sitting in my driveway.

A week later, a mechanic friend came over, and I asked him to look at my car. He went right under the dashboard, looked in a little fuse box, pulled out one particular fuse, and said, "Oh, the wire is broken."

Now I was mad. That little wire had kept me from receiving all the power of that engine. I couldn't go anywhere. He took a new fuse and plugged it in. I got in the car, turned the key, and *vrrrmmphh*, it revved right up, and I drove away. There had been plenty of power in the engine, but I couldn't go anywhere because a little 1/50th of an inch thick wire was disconnected.

You may think faith is a small thing. It is. He has done all the work. He has made it all available. But He requires you to believe, to really put your personal trust in Him, and then He will show you. A lot of people say, "Show me God, and I will believe." But God says this, "Believe in Me, and I will show you." When you do that, Jesus Christ shows you that He loves you. He has provided forgiveness and restoration, and you can actually know God as your dearest friend.

Day Twenty-Nine
His Golden Resurrection

> *...Which He worked in Christ when He raised Him from the dead and seated Him at His right hand in the heavenly places...And He put all things under His feet, and gave Him to be head over all things to the church, which is His body, the fullness of Him who fills all in all.*
>
> Ephesians 1:20, 22-23

The greatest demonstration of the power of God ever shown was the resurrection of Jesus Christ. Think of all the power it must have taken to create the universe, thrusting the planets and stars into orbit with all that fire, gas, and energy. God thrust out billions of stars and galaxies with His fingers. That was creating something out of nothing. Now that's power!

When God raised Jesus Christ from the dead, He was bringing forth life, not out of nothing, but out of death. That's what I love about the Lord's power—it's so wonderfully constructive. He takes the worst dead stuff and turns it into life, redeeming something bad, and making it into something wonderful.

Physical death is our worst enemy. It's going to get all of us. There is no escape except through Jesus Christ. We can die a lot of different ways, but death is what's going to get us in the end. Christ conquered it. He took this worst enemy of man, this thing that is going to kill us all, and He conquered it.

Paul asks, "*'O death, where is your sting?'...But thanks be to God, who gives us the victory through our Lord Jesus Christ*" (1 Corinthians 15:55 and 57). He conquered death because death could not hold Him down. It says in Acts 2: 24, "*whom God raised up, having loosed the pains of death, because it was not possible that He should be held by it.*"

Death could not hold Him down; He is the Son of God—God the Son.

Let's think for a minute about Jesus. He died on the cross, and the Bible says that He gave up His spirit saying, "*Father, 'into Your hands I commit My spirit'*" (Luke 23:46). His soul and spirit left His body, and His body was dead. Now we know that He was alive as He went into Hades and actually preached to the spirits there. He proclaimed the work that He was accomplishing to the believers and to the others (1 Peter 3:18-19). But His body was dead. His body hung limp on the cross. Scripture says, "*...He gave up His spirit*" (John 19:30).

Nicodemus and Joseph of Arimathea came and took His body down. They laid it in Joseph's tomb, and while His body was lying there in the tomb, it was lifeless. At that point, He couldn't use His hands to go out and touch people who needed healing as He had done so many times. He couldn't take food and multiply it to feed people. He couldn't use His mouth to speak those powerful words of truth and love that transformed so many people. He couldn't use His feet to walk miles and miles to be with people, embrace them, help them, and share with them.

But then something incredible happened. His mighty Spirit raised up His body from the dead. Now He could do all the things He had done before, and more. He revealed Himself to His disciples with many convincing proofs and with many different appearances after He rose from the dead (Acts 1:3).

Since Jesus ascended to heaven, His body on earth is His followers, you and I. Look at Ephesians 1:22-23, "*And He put all things under His feet, and gave Him to be head over all things to the church, which is His body, the fullness of Him who fills all in all.*" Of course, Jesus has His physical body that has been raised to heaven, but He has His earthly body right here, His followers, and the members of His church, those who believe in Him and love Him. In other words, there is an organic, powerful relationship between the Son of God, Jesus Christ, and His followers, us. He has given us His Holy Spirit if we believe in Him. He has placed His life into us. We have His thoughts through His Word. His Spirit flows into us. He is the head and the heart, and we are the members. His Holy Spirit is the flow of life. You could say the Holy Spirit is like the nervous system and the circulatory system of the body of Christ.

A very sad thing happens physically when someone gets into an accident that severs the spinal cord. Their body becomes paralyzed and lifeless because it's cut off from the brain. It no longer takes directions from the head and becomes useless to the person, even a burden, as it deteriorates and atrophies.

Similarly, it's sad when a member of Christ's body is not listening to Him, closing himself off from His Word and from His impulses. Sometimes, a brother closes himself off from the love, power, and blessing that Jesus wants to give him through unbelief and disobedience. It's especially sad when a person is separated from Jesus Christ, not receiving that wonderful, purposeful, abundant life of God. A person like that is lifeless spiritually. They are paralyzed and useless. God has a wonderful purpose and plan, but they're cut off from it without Christ.

I had a friend who was brought up in a good church, and he knew the Lord. God was a real part of his life. But as he got older, he turned his back on the Lord and became very rebellious. He even tried to lead a lot of us away from God. He was kind of a daredevil too and would do crazy stunts. One day, he was at a state park and decided to dive off a cliff into the water below. He didn't know there was a big rock a few feet below the surface, and when he dove off, he hit his head on that rock, severing his spinal cord. This guy who had been the most energetic, strong, vibrant fellow was now paralyzed for the rest of his life. But you know what? He realized what a fool he had been by turning his back on God, running and rebelling from Him. His own body was an illustration of what his life had become apart from Christ. But then he gave his life back to Jesus. His body is paralyzed, but he is alive! He has become a great witness and minister for the Lord. God has an incredible plan. One day, when this brief life is over, he is going to get a new body for eternity.

There is an eternity, my friend, and it's <u>forever</u>. FOREVER! That's something you don't want to mess up. God has a wonderful plan for our lives, and His number one priority is that we be joined with Christ, receiving His love, His Spirit, His wisdom, and His power. He wants you to know Him and fellowship with Him and do His will. What is His will? That you and I would be part of that full expression of Jesus here on earth.

Day Thirty
Spending Our Father's Wealth

> *...Far above all principality and power and might and dominion, and every name that is named, not only in this age but also in that which is to come. And He put all things under His feet, and gave Him to be head over all things to the church, which is His body, the fullness of Him who fills all in all.*
>
> *Ephesians 1:21-23*

We are His body, the fullness of Him who fills all in all. He fills us. He wants to empower us and fill us with His Spirit so that corporately we can express Him to the world. You have a part if you are a believer. This world desperately needs to see Jesus Christ. And our head, Christ, who is in heaven, needs a full body to work with.

He doesn't need just a few members. He doesn't want just three teeth so He can smile a toothless smile at people, or a couple of toes, a few fingernails, or maybe one eyeball. He doesn't want to be a body that is not whole, that is not complete. Yet, many times, we look at the body of Christ and see that different parts have dropped out or are not functioning. That's sad. The Lord wants to fill us. That's why Paul prayed that we would know His power, His presence, and His glory working in and through our lives. Only then, with a full body of believers, will there be a full expression of Christ.

How do we receive the fullness of His presence and the power of Jesus Christ that He wants to give us? Well, Ephesians 1:19 says it's "*toward us who believe*" who know what is the "*exceeding greatness of His power.*" It's so simple! By faith, receive. Our faith in Him triggers that awesome power. It activates the power of Jesus Christ on our behalf. It's kind of like the switch that activates a powerful generator, or a button that activates a nuclear reactor. It seems so small and insignificant, but it's vital to engaging the power supply. Faith might seem like a little thing, and it is! The power is not faith. The power is what faith is tapping into. Through faith, you can have this awesome power of Jesus Christ to overcome whatever keeps you from representing Him.

Remember when Jesus went to that funeral service for Lazarus (John 11:1-44)? Everyone was weeping, singing sad songs, and wailing. Then Jesus came, and He started crying too. He told Mary and Martha, "Believe in Me, because I'm going to do something incredible." They replied, "Well, yeah, we think so, sometime in the future." He said, "Didn't I tell you that if you believe Me, you would see the glory of God?" Then Jesus ruined the funeral by going over to the grave and shouting, "Lazarus! Come on out!" Lazarus came out, hobbling in his grave clothes, and everyone was stunned. Jesus' power is stunning. And the Bible says that many believed.

Sometimes I think the body of Christ is a little bit like sleeping Lazarus or dead Lazarus. It's as if Jesus is saying to us, "People come forth, rise up!" Through His power and His Spirit, we can rise up and people will say, "Wow, the Lord is real." That's tremendous!

Ephesians 1:20-21 says God raised up Christ and seated Him at His right hand in the heavenly places "*far above all principality and power and might and dominion, and every name that is named, not only in this age but also in that which is to come.*"

Satan had the power of death, but Christ conquered him. Satan is one of those principalities referred to here. Sometimes when we hear the name Satan, we shudder. But why should we? We have the name of Jesus!

Sometimes we meet someone who is into witchcraft or into a cult, the occult, or some terrible sin, and we're afraid and think, "Oh no!" Hey, you're into Jesus—they're the ones who should be going, "Oh no!" You have Christ! His name is far above every name that is named. He is powerful far beyond Satan; He makes Satan look like an ant, just a small creature. Christ is the Creator. The Holy Spirit is the Creator, and He lives in you!

My daughter was on a basketball team that played this team with really nice uniforms; they were looking good! But my daughter's team won 83 to 13—it was a boring game. That's like Jesus against Satan—it's a wipe out. It's not even fun to watch what the Lord can do to the devil. Jesus Christ is in our lives, the power of God. I love what Ephesians 1: 22 says, "*He put all things under His feet, and gave Him to be head over all things to the church...*" Look at that. He put all things under His feet, Jesus' feet. Since Jesus rose from the dead and ascended to heaven, everything is underneath Him. Everything is subject to Him. He proved He is Lord of all.

Notice it doesn't say He put all things under His head. What is the lowest, most humble part of His body? Well, the lowest part of my body is my feet, my toes. Jesus put all things under His feet. That includes every one of us who are part of His body. In other words, He is over all, He is the head, and He is Lord of all. Therefore, anything that would try to rise up and pull us down to defeat cannot succeed because Jesus' power puts it under us. We look to Him and we trust in Him. He said, "*In the world you will have tribulation; but be of good cheer, I have overcome the world*" (John 16:33). How did He overcome the world? He's God. How do we overcome the world? By believing in Him. He said to be of good cheer for He has overcome the world. "Well, that's nice for You, Lord, but what about me?" As believers, you're part of His body. He will give you His victory when you trust Him, when you believe in Him.

Again, it's through simple faith that we trust and commune with Him. I had this car that sometimes wouldn't start. It was off and on, sometimes it worked, and sometimes it didn't. I would go out each day, open the hood and wiggle the battery cables. They were loose, and like a dummy, I never got it fixed. But when it wouldn't start, I would just wiggle the battery cable, which tightened the connection, and then the car would start right up. The power was always there, but sometimes the connection was loose.

Friends, keep your connection to Jesus tight. Faith is not just a one-time thing. It is maintained through constant, daily fellowship. Every day we need to tune in and trust. Yes, salvation is that one time reception, but the relationship keeps growing. You don't have His power apart from Him—you have to be hooked up. And that comes from faith, trust, and prayer. It's all there for you. Depend on it.

Epilogue

Friends, for thirty days now, we have been learning about the unsearchable riches of Christ. We have discovered that because of Jesus Christ and His unspeakable gift of His life for us, God has deposited unlimited riches of strength, wisdom, and love into the spiritual accounts of each of us. Now it is up to you to draw by faith from your heavenly Father's account. You need to do so every single day. Get out your checkbook and utilize those riches for God's glory. Every check is signed by Jesus!

Endnotes

[1] William Barclay, *Letter to the Galatians and Ephesians*, Westminster John Knox Press, Philadelphia, Pennsylvania, 1976, pg. 85.
[2] G. Coleman Luck, *First Corinthians*, Moody Press, Chicago, Illinois, 1958, pgs. 36-37.
[3] J. Vernon McGee, *Matthew, Volume 1*, Thru the Bible Books, Pasadena, California, pgs. 184-185.
[4] Paul Lee Tan, *Signs of the Times*, Bible Communications, Inc., Garland, Texas, 1979, pg. 510.

About the Author

WAYNE TAYLOR, the senior pastor of Calvary Fellowship in Seattle/Mountlake Terrace, Washington, is a stimulating and practical teacher who relates biblical truths to the needs of today. He is the featured speaker on the radio program, *Consider Jesus,* and the author of four books: *He Dwelt Among Us: A Daily Devotional Through the Gospel of John; The Civil War Within: Biblical "Facts of Life" in the Struggle for Spiritual Growth* (a study through Romans chapters 1-8); *Practical Christian Living* (a study through Romans chapters 12-13); and *The Unsearchable Riches of Christ.* Wayne lives in Seattle with his wife Cathy and their four children.